Dear Ruth –

Happy Birthday!

Edna and
Shimshon Inbal

Anthology of
Modern Hebrew Poetry

IN TWO VOLUMES

SELECTED BY S.Y. PENUELI

AND A. UKHMANI

Volume One

INSTITUTE FOR THE TRANSLATION OF HEBREW LITERATURE

 AND

ISRAEL UNIVERSITIES PRESS, JERUSALEM, 1966

Israel Universities Press
is a subsidiary publishing imprint for certain books,
either published in the original language,
or translations of works not in the exact sciences,
of the
ISRAEL PROGRAM FOR SCIENTIFIC TRANSLATIONS
P. O. BOX 7145 / Jerusalem / Israel

This book has been composed in Monophoto Times New Roman at IPST,
Printed by S. Monson and Bound by Wiener Bindery Ltd.,
Jerusalem, Israel, 1966

To the great sorrow of all who knew him
Professor S. Y. Penueli passed away shortly before this Anthology went to press.
The Institute for the Translation of Hebrew Literature
wishes to record its gratitude for his important contribution
to the planning and production of this Anthology.

The Institute expresses its sincere thanks to Professor Daniel A. Fineman,
Chairman of the Department of English at Tel Aviv University,
for his help in evaluating the translations.

For permission to use copyright material in this volume
the Institute for the Translation of Hebrew Literature expresses its thanks to:
Mrs. Mania Bialik for the poems of H. N. Bialik
Mr. Avraham Wilenski for the poems of Sh. Tchernikhovsky
Mrs. Alisa Steinberg for the poems of Y. Steinberg
Mrs. Miriam Cahan for the poems of Y. Cahan
Mrs. Ada Silberstein for the poems of Y. Fichman
Mrs. Annie Lamdan for the poems of Y. Lamdan
Mr. Shmuel Shimoni for the poems of D. Shimoni
Mr. David Rimon for the poems of I. Z. Rimon
Mrs. Shoshana Blumstein-Sela for the poems of Rachel

Table of Contents to Volume One

Introduction

BY S. Y. PENUELI

MODERN Hebrew poetry marks the renaissance of the Hebrew nation. Pre-vious attempts made during the period of the *Haskalah* (the Jewish Cultural Emancipation) had all proved unsuccessful, and their failure was due to a variety of causes. The poetry was too self-imitative to arouse the dormant strains of music in the language, and consequently it remained pseudo-biblical and unoriginal. Moreover, it was too emulative of other poetry, striving to adopt forms that were essentially alien to its own spirit, and thus it became pseudo-classical and barren, unable to reproduce its own genre. For a renais-sance cannot merely imitate works of the past—whether its own past or that of others!—but it must attest to the mighty spirit that pervaded its past, mir-roring its cultural and spiritual heritage.

It was Bialik who engendered the renaissance of Hebrew poetry. He was preceded by two modern trends in the poetry of the West: that of Baudelaire, the lineage of which harks back to Wagner, Nietzsche, Schopenhauer and Kant, then further back to ancient Greece and the Dionysian musicalism; and that of Whitman, whose genealogical tree sent out far-reaching branches to enfold in a mighty embrace the wide New World, with its many peoples, unite them in the spirit of pantheism, democracy and human love—a tree whose roots drank of the living streams of the Quakers, fed from the sources of the very Scriptures, in their various versions, from the Reformation to the parent-stream of the Hebrew Bible itself.

Yet Bialik formed no alliance with either of these trends. As his essays show, he evolved his own original concepts of the nature of poetry and its creative processes. His essays, in fact, contain the quintessence of all theories of modern poetry. They contain a prognosis, as it were, of the future directions that poetry was to take—Hermetism, Expressionism, musicalism, imagism and other ex-periments that poetry was due to make. Yet he himself neither clung to the 'old' nor veered towards the 'new', but simply walked the road of poetry itself. In his poem *All Alone,* one feels that the very rhythm of the first two lines expresses the poet's scorn for those who are drawn to the 'new' poetry:

] 1 [

The wind took them, the light swept them along,
The morning of their lives sang with a new song.

The anapaest stress falling heavily on the word 'new' lends it a clumsiness rather than dignity and draws attention to the paradox inherent in the juxta-position of 'new' and 'song'. This necessarily arouses in the mind of the reader, accustomed as he is to contrasting associations, the possibility that there might also exist an 'old poetry', which is an absurdity. This 'new' poetry, which seems to appear at the window with the early morning light—how insignificant it becomes when overshadowed by the greatness of man's loneliness enfolded by the sheltering, broken wing of the Divine Presence.

Bialik regarded all those who went after this 'light', forsaking the traditional *Bet-Midrash* (Jewish house of learning), as heirs benefiting from the labours of others, who either inherited the 'light' flashed by strangers, or dissipated the heritage of their own fathers. Bialik himself was no inheritor in this sense. A renaissance does not consist merely in taking possession of a heritage. It is a spell cast over the spirit, which assumes a new form in man, and there it lies imprisoned, languishing in captivity and yearning for release.

Not by chance did I find light,
Nor inherited it at life's start.
But I pried it out of my rock and my stone,
And hewed it from out of my heart.

Never before had Hebrew poetry been charged with such a wondrous com-bination of prophetic utterance—harsh and rugged, as if rough-hewn from the very rocks of the wilderness—with the musical strains of clear-toned anapaest rhythms and restrained onomatopoeia. It is no longer the moral reproof as such that strikes the ear. The poem itself embodies human ethics and human integrity. Man's heart is the rock at which the poet hews, and from which the truth emerges. And just as the rock stands fast, immutable, so does Bialik's poetic truth remain firm-set throughout.

Bialik is the poet of the Hebrew renaissance not merely by virtue of the fact that his poems express the national revival—for this can be manifested out-side the realm of poetry—but because it was he who brought to life the forces that had lain dormant in the Hebrew language ever since the language and nation had been formed and taken shape; for the two were created at one and the same time. Though he devoted his energies to such major poetic works as *Ha-Berecha* ('The Pool'), *Metei Midbar* ('The Desert Dead'), or *Megillat Ha-Esh* ('The Scroll of Fire'), he is nonetheless essentially a lyrical poet. His lyrical self transcends all subjectivity as he wields complete sway over words, forcing them to surrender their musical magic. And since music is the universe expressed in song, the national themes of Bialik's poetry achieve a universal symbolism; their apparent significance is of a personal or national character, yet their underlying meaning is of world-wide import. Thus the language of Hebrew poetry again becomes a universal force, filled with artistic content as well as with national significance.

A tendril dropped to a fence and slept—
So I sleep too:
The fruit fell. With my trunk and branches, what
Have I to do?

The twig that floated down to a fence and slumbered arouses a host of associations in an endless chain, charged with an infinite variety of symbols that probe ever deeper and deeper. Those familiar with the poet's personal life-story will see in this twig Bialik the man, who feels alone and cut off from the main stem now that his poetic fruit has fully ripened. Others, acquainted with the course of his work, will suddenly be struck by the astounding fact that this was the last poem he wrote before he was overwhelmed by the comparative silence—the severance from the parent-trunk—which marked a complete change in his work to the end. Of deeper significance is the symbol by which the twig is suggestive of the fate of the poet's people—the Jewish nation that yielded to mankind, the parent-trunk, its finest and most mature fruit, namely the Bible, only to be shed and remain severed from the trunk while others continued to partake of the fruit. Of even deeper significance still is the twig's symbolizing the fate of man in general: man, whose spirit is fully ripened, employs this very spirit in preparing his own extinction and increasingly severs himself from the instinct of survival that is the very essence of existence. Thus the national poet has become the poet of Man, mirroring all existence in his own image, and his voice, which sings the world's song, echoes the whole of the universe. His lyrical 'I' is no longer the subjective 'I', but the 'I' of millions.

Bialik's *magical* poetry, however, was of relatively short duration, lasting from 1891 till about 1911, when it underwent a significant change. This change

] 3 [

might well be compared to that which transformed his people's poetry and literature in general. His early poetry had a magically musical quality, and so had early Hebrew poetry. Incidentally, the rhythmic properties of biblical poetry have not been as fully investigated as has, say, the scansion of ancient Greek verse. What, however, characterises the rhythm of biblical poetry is its Hebrew parallelism. It may well be that this rhythmic parallelism rests on a deeper, sub-stratic resonantal foundation, perceptible only to the well-attuned ear. An example that readily offers itself is in the first line of poetry in the Book of Job, which comes immediately after the narrative opening: 'Let the day perish wherein I was born, and the night in which it was said, There is a man child conceived.' In the original:

YOVAD YOM IVALED BO VE-LAILA AMAR HORA GAVER.

Apart from being parallelistic, the verse has also a pure trochaic metre.

As we have mentioned, Bialik's poetry took a most significant turn in 1911. It emerges from the confines of the magical property of words to the realm of poetic vision, where idea takes precedence over art. It exchanges tonal music for biblical parallelism. It has become charged with a nostalgia for childhood, yet is resigned to the impossibility of returning to the magic of animistic childhood. It begins to doubt the power of words; at the same time it is a song of praise sung to the meek and silent of this world, those 'mute of soul, who weave the pattern of their lives in secret', or as he puts it in his poem *May my Lot be with Them.*

> The votaries of quiet beauty,
> The priests of divine silence.

This change in his poetry also expresses the poet's changed attitude to reality, which cannot stand up to the test of human ethics and morality when left to the vagaries of nature alone; it must needs be selectively guided by poetry, enhanced by art and elevated by man's spiritual forces.

In 'My Father', one of the poems that form Bialik's last poetic work, 'Orphanhood', his magical language has assumed rhetorical overtones. Animistic childhood is now seen as a reproduction in which the wisdom of maturity is blended, the imagery and the treatment of the theme idealized. The father-image is seen as 'the head of a martyr', as a dismembered bust, and the unseen heart 'moans like a wondrous violin'. Here, the poet looks back in retrospective wonder at the strange course of his life: his poetic course was identical with that of the poetry of his people, and underwent the same changes, yet in a far shorter span. The rare combination of extreme realism and extreme transcendentalism which marks his poetry is an ontogenetic reflection of the poet's lyrical self, symbolizing the polygenesis, the lyrical 'I' of the Hebrew nation.

Like Bialik, Shaul Tchernikhovsky, his contemporary, shared in the renascence of the Hebrew language and was responsible for important innovations in the content and form of Hebrew poetry. Long was the poetic road he followed, yet unlike Bialik, his road was not fraught with such spiritual crises. The magical depths of the Hebrew language were not revealed to Tchernikhovsky in the same way as they were to Bialik; hence he was not affected by any dispelling of the magic, which may frequently doom the poet to silence. Nor was Judaism revealed to him in all its amplitude and depth, in all its wide reaches between realism and transcendence. The Hebrew poetry of the *Haskala* revealed Judaism to him in its narrowest aspects, and he did not have Bialik's power of widening these narrow straits. He therefore roamed the distant reaches beyond the realms of Judaism, bringing back to Hebrew rich foreign spoils, both in his original poems and in his translations. In his translations he opened up to Hebrew poetry the riches of the four corners of the earth: Homer's *Iliad* and *Odyssey* from the South, the Finnish epic *Kalevala* from the North, *Hiawatha* from the West, the Babylonian epic legends from the East. His original poetry, too, was nurtured from ancient sources: the pristine, pre-monotheistic period of the ancient Hebrews of Canaan, the Dionysian concepts he had discovered in the writings of Nietzsche. His firm poetic spirit, however, reinforced as it was by the pristine ingenuousness of the ancients and proof against any disabused rationalization, was able to overcome all apparent contradictions and weld them together into one poetic whole—a main stem whose roots drank from different springs.

The drunken dance of the king with the throng of prophets in his poem 'The King' is highly reminiscent of that of Dionysus in Nietzsche's 'Birth of Tragedy'. But there is an essential difference, for 'The King' also conveys the original Hebrew prophetic spirit. This prophecy, in its earliest purity, does not set out to lay down moral and didactic motifs, but is an expression of man's yearning for the sublime, a yearning that can never be fully satisfied by dint of human effort; it is, as it were, a universal, boundless zeal, of which morality is but an after-growth, a kind of hand-hold on the endless ascent to the infinite heights of man's spirit, amidst a positive, practical reality. Tchernikhovsky's

] 5 [

'King', too, after having discarded all those earthly and individual attributes that distinguish man from man and from all other creatures, is seized by a Dionysian fervour, a universal intoxication, and becomes the Prophet, the Lord's anointed:

> And the spirit of the Lord alighted upon His anointed,
> And he too prophesied in the midst of the camp.
> Then he became one with the universe and the fullness thereof,
>
> One small spark in the infinite world,
> Loving and cleaving to all of Creation.
> And he fell down naked all that day and all that night.
> Naked... naked... naked.

His poem 'Death of Tammuz', though based on an ancient pagan rite, hardly advocates a reversion to idolatry. It rather seeks to alleviate the plight of modern man, give him re-access to the limitless possibilities known as 'miracles', of which modern civilization has bereft him, to free him from the limitations imposed by a modern science, no less deterministic than mythical fate and the Olympian *Moira*. The Tammuz is none other than a symbolic projection of these possibilities, failing which, the human soul is defective, limited by such biological functions as birth, death and reproduction:

> Come forth and weep, ye daughters of Zion,
> At the sorrow of the world, bereft of miracle
> At the sorrow of a world wounded in soul.
> The bright Tammuz, yea the bright Tammuz is dead.

It was Tchernikhovsky who introduced into Hebrew poetry such European forms as the sonnet, ballad and idyll. His ballads conform to all the requirements this form imposes, namely the air of mystery, the fateful event where man meets his true self, and the lilting rhythms. *The Bells, The Last Khuzar* and *Ballad of the Beehive,* which appear in this collection, point to his strict adherence to ballad form. His idylls, too, conform to the rigid demands exacted by this form of poetry: they sound the echo of the mighty world as faintly heard in everyday life, the great wonder of man's leading this life in tranquillity and wisdom, his yearnings refined and purified in the calm flow of the hexameters.

Zalman Shneour's poetry is essentially intellectual. It was he, in fact, who elevated modern Hebrew poetry to the peaks of contemporary European pessimism. Lacking Bialik's magical gift of language, or Tchernikhovsky's ingenuousness and understanding, Shneour's poetry may tend to be rated as secondary, in that it seems to give thought precedence to poetic form rather than fuse the two. The poet, however, fully alive to these shortcomings, turned them to advantage. Sharpness of wit, forcefulness and intellectual zest gain complete mastery in his poems and frequently coerce the language, as it were, into becoming adequate enough to express his contemplative and revolutionary ideas. His poems, devoid of all nostalgic yearning and romantic weakness, acclaim the genius of man carving out his future destiny. He admires this human genius in Judaism and what Judaism has produced, as in 'Deuteronomy', where:

> Light chases the shadows,
>   Precepts burst into song,
> Narrative turns into poem,
>   The prophet, not judge, rebukes wrong.
>
> The nation's heart is pulsating
>   Its lawyers and shepherd and seer,
> With flute and with timbrel proclaiming
>   'O earth, O heaven, give ear!'

and in *Spartacüs,* too, he extols the heights which the human spirit has attained.

Yet Shneour's very aversion to the romantic is in itself a kind of romanticism, common to every poet, where it is not merely a contemporary appearance or an historical episode, but an immortal urge in man. His 'inverted' romanticism actually romanticizes human progress:

> I care not to return to idyllic cities
>   Floundering in medieval mire...
> Only in this mature world let me live
>   Where the corn stands proud and golden,
> Where the ripe stands proud and golden,
>
> Only in this world with its mighty storms
>   With its joyful certainties and doubts
> On the threshold of discovery or death...
>   Where disbelief challenges the heavens.

There may you find me in darkness, yet aflame,
   On the ladder that reaches up to God.

It is this mature romanticism, with all its fiery unorthodoxy and 'gay wisdom', that has placed Shneour in opposition to another kind of romanticism—that of modernism in poetry, in all its manifestations of Hermetism, Surrealism and spontaneity. Against all these he appeals in 'Stop Playing':

Stop playing with words, you fools!
   Each true word is a sharp tooth.
Yours are decayed and crooked.
   They will never grow again.

Yaakov Cahan, David Shimoni and Yaakov Fichman were contemporaries of Bialik, Tchernikhovsky and Shneour, yet were not overshadowed by their greatness. Each followed his own distinctive path and drew on his own individual power. Yaakov Cahan turned to the medium of the prose poem, which he imbued with messianic motifs, and also to poetic drama. He drew much of his inspiration from Bialik's *Scroll of Fire,* from Rabindranath Tagore and from Goethe's dramatic works, he himself having translated *Faust* and *Iphigenia in Tauris* into Hebrew. David Shimoni devoted himself largely to idylls of the new life taking shape in the re-awakened Land of Israel, which in itself was far from idyllic; hence, Shimoni's idylls were essentially remote from the basic concept of the idyll and bore but a superficial resemblance to it. Both Yaakov Fichman and Yaakov Steinberg were distinctively lyrical as well as distinctively personal poets—the former out of his implicit faith in lyricism, which he regarded as the very essence of all poetry, and the latter by dint of his forceful personality. It was this personality that weighed its generation in the balance, and imposed on itself the rigid task of epitomizing all that was good and evil in the restlessness that has marked the Jewish people at all times.

It was in lyricism that Yaakov Fichman saw the salvation of the world and of man, the supreme test of the nation and of the individual. All other forms of creative art are of value only insofar as they attest to the proliferation of the lyricist, who frequently is bound to transcend the borders of lyricism to seek an outlet for his abundant creative energies. Lyricism is man's ultimate perfection, the final embodiment of his spiritual aspirations, the sublimation of all thought and labour. In *'Noah',* man finds no peace in the new, flood-washed land, where Spring flowers in the smiling valleys, the dim forests and the rejoicing hills, for he hears the dying moan of the world that has perished in the depths of that same flood as watered the land and made it flower. As if to cover up the shadow cast by the dead world, he takes his spade and plants a vineyard, not that he may be drunk and forget, but rather:

A shadow on the shade of a world that has died...
He dug a grave for the shadow and covered it.

It is this 'shadow' that is the essence of Fichman's lyricism, whether in his early collection of poems *Shadows on the Fields,* or in his last work *Edge of the Field.* It is calm, subdued and gentle. It is mellowed with overtones of deep sadness, a twilight air of resignation. Yet it is this shadow that overlies other shades; this resignation that subdues mighty aspirations. The poet's heart made great demand, but his lips refrained from clamour, as if restrained by that ancient biblical truth 'The Lord cometh not in tumult.' The cry that welled up within him was stilled and muted in gentle tones, and the flames of his inner fire were covered with 'shadow', like Moses in his poem *Nevo:*

He whose heart made great demand
Inherits but a little land...

For it is not because 'his strength was abated' that Moses does not cross into the Promised Land, but because he bears the Promised Land within him, deeply enfolded in his heart; the Promised Land for him is not merely a geographical terrain. Similarly in Fichman's poetry, the greatness is closed up within the heart, reluctant to burst forth, as it were, and there it lies eternally flowering in silence and in shade.

Of Yaakov Steinberg, Bialik wrote in his essay *Our Young Poetry:* 'His wings touch the stratosphere and he gazes down from on high. His flight is straight and wide-sweeping, aspiring to great distances.' This appraisal is somewhat surprising if related to the works of Steinberg which appeared before Bialik published this essay in 1907, but seems to be very true in regard to what Steinberg wrote subsequently. In retrospect, in fact, Bialik's remark seems to be a prognosis, for Steinberg indeed observes man from 'on high' and steers his poetry to great, distant flights. Nor does he sing of mere man, but of the *excellence of man.* And in order to attain this, he describes a wide sweeping arc, which keeps him out of touch with what is taking place in contemporary

Hebrew and modern poetry, but which causes him to alight upon Hebrew poetry's great past, the biblical past.

Steinberg fully realised that in order to attain to biblical heights, a poet must guard against merely imitating scriptural forms and patterns, just as the scriptures themselves were not imitative of the oriental modes of their environment. The Bible engendered the single, self-contained line of poetry, the intensive line that attests to the intensity of the spiritual epic. And it is by virtue of these powerful, single lines that the Bible has maintained its artistic quality throughout the ages, embodying the quintessence of art and faith, spiritual vigour and wisdom. Were it not for these powerfully poetic lines, the Bible might well have been contained in one small book, replaceable by other versions at different times, and ultimately divorced from life's truth. But the great, single line of Biblical verse has found no substitute in world literature, and thus it has retained the spirit of man's greatness, which cannot be exchanged for any other greatness. It is to such lines that Steinberg's poetry strives to attain, and it is such lines that he creates with a biblical force that does not savour of pseudo-biblicalism. He sings of the rain:

> Suddenly a heavy rain lashed the earth
> > Telling of truth and mystery.

and it is the song of a man who has returned to his ancient, arid homeland, which gave birth to 'man's excellence' in the distant past, and which in the not too-distant future will be peopled with a *small mighty nation*. Of this life-giving rain he writes:

> It runs its pure course from the lofty sky
> > Bringing the word of God from heaven.

When the poet has aged prematurely and is filled with life's wisdom, he still employs the biblical line to probe man's hidden depths from 'on high':

> I have laboured with the many who are confused
> > To find this refuge where we need not fear,
> The weeping of our flesh and their hidden truth.

It is the same line, charged with the excellence of man, that the poet transfers to his prose, which is essay-like, biblical and poetic at one and the same time. Yet its essay-like quality does not emanate from any tradition of Montaigne, nor is its biblical quality drawn from scriptural patterns. Both these traditions are fused into an original, direct and broad-sweeping emanation that rises to the greatest heights.

Bialik was the harbinger of modern Hebrew lyrical poetry. In his essay *Revelation and Allusion in Language,* the revelation of this poetry appeared to him as a 'Sweet Dread', where man faces the test of peering into the yawning abyss of his own self. The message he brought materialized in the poets that came after him, some of them of his own generation. For Bialik, poetry was a riddle, as it were, to which he sought the solution; solution-less poetry was for him a most 'serious game', which only children or poets that had not yet emerged from childhood could afford to play, and the game ceased the moment their childhood had departed. But modern lyricism encompasses *mature* man and grows ever stronger by dint of the force of language, endeavouring 'to extract the maximum of hints and allusions from a minimum of words.' And since the initial growth of language itself is correlated to the growth of a nation and of man himself, it is by its very nature bound up with childhood and does not, therefore, have to invoke the childlike qualities in the personality of the poet. Poetry thus becomes a creation of language, stimulating the urge towards growth, which is a quality of childhood amidst the maturity of mankind, and revitalizing its desire for progress.

One year after Bialik wrote *A Twig Floated Down* (1911), Avraham Ben-Yitzhak wrote his 'Psalm':

Rarely does one raise one's jewel-like soul
To catch the sunlight's rainbow-coloured world.

The poet stresses 'rarely', for very few and rare indeed are those who raise their souls. As a rule, it is the soul that raises man, and when the soul bears him, the complexes of the soul also bear him and darken his spirit. But when man bears his soul, it becomes clear and untroubled like 'a jewel'—a world infused with its own sunlight. When a man lifts his soul, it becomes a *world* that engenders upward growth, unlimited by any horizontal plane. All things and deeds develop and are borne aloft on the blind wheel of chance and change, without beginning or end or interrelation. It is only man's poetry that does not 'develop' thus, but remains constant and firm, as a sentinel of the world:

When a star falls
A shout of fear

Rises heavenward
  From the depths of hell.
The star falls into your soul
  And is snuffed in its depths.
But next morn you float
  On the surface of the deep
Spreading your heavens
  The great sun in your hands
—Till evening.

It is man who spreads out his deep heavens and holds his sun in his hand, nor can his heavens and sun exist independently of him. These are created by words, by language that becomes poetry by dint of the eternal youth inherent in words and by virtue of their eternal restlessness.

Avraham Ben-Yitzhak infused Hebrew poetry with this restlessness, which has not subsided ever since. It partook of Western influences, as in the poetry of David Vogel and Avigdor Hameiri; it imbibed those of the East, as in the poems of Yocheved Bat-Miriam; it became charged with the *sefirot* emanations of Hebrew mysticism, as well as with universal Platonic thought; it became imbued with philosophical religiosity in the hands of Avraham Regelson, and with mystic religiosity in the hands of I. Z. Rimon.

Thus poetry broke faith with nature. It perforce had to withdraw from nature and turn back to man, again refining itself to the point of lyricism. The nineteenth-century cycle of intuitions (as Croce terms the interrelation of art, thought and deed) had now come full circle. Nineteenth-century poetry, which had stimulated nineteenth-century thought—the hope of human and humanistic progress—which in turn had stimulated nineteenth-century endeavour, culminated in poetic disillusionment: man does not bear his soul and does not spread out his heavens, nor does he hold his sun in his hand. On the contrary: man is sustained by his soul, his heavens are lost, and his sun is merely a source of energy, wastefully spent on maintaining man's animal life on the surface of the earth. Man no longer adequately fulfils his destiny as man. His art, which is intrinsically near to nature, instead of bringing man closer to himself, brings him closer to nature. What is needed is a new poetry, more autonomous yet more dependent at the same time: more autonomous, in that it makes is own laws and prescribes its own rhythms, free of all repetitive, constrictive metre; yet dependent on other intuitions, which it stimulates but does not assimilate. For poetry may not replace intuition, nor may it turn it into thought; otherwise it would not fulfil its self-imposed function of stimulating this intuitive thought. Similarly, poetry may not assume the burden of action, lest it become devoid of its intuitive distinctiveness, for its task it is to protect human action against the evils of inertia. The poet's task is but to sing; he is the blacksmith who forges the language, who smelts the words in fire to soften them, cools them in water to temper them, and then hammers them into coiled steel springs which launch man's soul to unknown heights, burning with unquenchable fires—as one allusion sets another afire, image lights up image, and idea flashes from idea.

The Hebrew nation, aware of the imminent approach of its new era of self-redemption, of intuitive deed, preceded this with a new intuitive poetry. And this new intuitive poetry was kindled at the still-smouldering fires of the biblical poetic heritage, was fanned by the strong winds that blew from the West and burst into flame. Avraham Ben-Yitzhak sought to release this new poetry from the encumbrances of easy solutions:

> Blessed are those who sow and do not reap,
> Because they wander far...
> Blessed are those who know that their heart cries out in the desert
> While on their lips silence flowers...

Thus, Ben-Yitzhak returned Hebrew poetry to its point of departure, free of all non-poetic ballast. But poetry cannot remain there for long. Even Imagism sought some 'object' which would justify the freedom of the imagery, such as the emotional-aesthetic complexes that release man from the captivity of the conventional. Impressionism, too, embarked for destinations that were beyond the realms of 'pure' poetry, such as pacifism and the brotherhood of mankind. All the more so biblical poetry, which never set out to nurture the aesthetic *per se*. Hebrew poetry was thus to be tossed by all these winds and trends and currents, to undergo *the struggle between original and foreign influences,* the struggle between *personal demands* and the *demands of literary modes.* The waves of this new poetry were to soar high, and its pure skies were to be engraved with the poetic figures of Uri Zvi Greenberg, Yitzhak Lamdan, Avraham Shlonsky and Natan Alterman. These waves were to clash with one another, perilously or in triumph.

Uri Zvi Greenberg's early verse of the '20's is associated with the German Expressionism of the time, wherein he found some projection of the biblical Hebrew expressionism conveyed in the Book of Ezekiel. He also caught the distant echo of the poetry of Walt Whitman, who seemed to him closer to Mount Sinai than to Mt. Olympus. Greenberg, who was of Hassidic origins, had, also, imbibed much of its ecstatic heritage. Thus armed, he set out to create for Hebrew poetry a new muse—a Tenth Muse, as he called it in his expressionist manifestos—divorced from European art, from Greek origins and musical rhythms; a muse that was harnessed to the fiery chariot of prophetic vision and messianic idea, both to be fulfilled through the immigration of Jewish pioneers to the Land of Israel and the establishment of the Third Kingdom of Israel. Greenberg's expressionism, however, underwent the same fate as that of the expressionism in Germany, the country of his birth. This expressionism sought to accomplish two objects that were mutually irreconcilable, namely New Man and a New Poetic Form. But this New Man had to be educated—whether to the fraternity of man, or democracy, or pacifism, or socialism, or communism— as advocated by the various European expressionists —or to a Hebrew renascence, pioneering self-fulfilment, Jewish statehood, or a renewal of the covenant with nature in the homeland—according to the individual dream of each Hebrew expressionist poet. Both the former and the latter could be conveyed only by a poetry that was communicative, objective, close to nature and to reality, intelligible and conformist. The poet may be head and shoulders *above his fellow-men* by virtue of his power of expression, his depth of feeling and strength of will, but he may not be *foreign to his fellow-men,* worlds apart from them, nor speak a language that is strange and incomprehensible to them. Thus there arose a contradiction between the *Aesthetic Idea* and the *Intellectual Idea*—which are irreconcilable, according to Kant's *Critique of Pure Reason.*

Greenberg's Tenth Muse could not endure, nor could the poet abide by it for long. The European expressionists very soon sought to become integrated into national, social and political movements and either adapted their poetry accordingly, or went over to extreme modernism, which is in no way related to any intellectual idea. Greenberg likewise sought this integration in the Jewish national, Zionist and pioneering movements, inspired with the ideal of Jewish statehood. His outright expressionism gave way to the national need. Yet his poetry still remained imbued with its distinctive activism, ecstasy and explosiveness of expression, which kindled in the hearts of many Jews the burning desire to fulfil their inevitable destiny of returning to their homeland from their European exile. The nation had already accomplished its task in the diaspora, its 'ambassadorial mission'—as Greenberg put it—of saying 'No' to a Europe that had become neurotic and filled with self-hate on account of its Jews. The time had now come for the Jewish nation to leave this Europe, the dread scene of *'Streets of the River'*, and return to the land that is its be-all and end-all, its spiritual and temporal homeland, of whose transcendence Greenberg sings in his *Song to Heaven:*

Not the language of the lowlands is the language
　　of our heart, our soul, our blood;
And we breathe—alive—not the air of this present,
　　but the air of our ancient days
Above the treetops of the usual and all the mountain
　　peaks of dailiness.
For in our depths there lives the song of the heavenly
　　ones,
Our shoulders tell the secret of the clipping of our
　　wings.

Yet Israel is also the nation's earthly homeland, of which the poet sings in *Song to the Earth:*

We shall not lift our eyes towards the heavens—
　　we are not the sons of giants, nor their daughters.
Who imprinted in our soul this fruitless yearning
　　for the sky?
All that is lost, all that exists in truth, in love,
　　in piercing pain,
Exists here in this lower world:
Here our mother bore us in pain, and here our father
　　ate the first apple;
Here we poured out good words, casting them into
　　bitter thoughts,
Myrrh and wine in a thousand poems to flowering love.
Here, from a neighbouring, lowly rock
　　we struck a spark of fire,
And here we raised the banner of rebellion...

Thus the poet has rediscovered himself and reverted to his origins, freed from the influences of Whitman and the expressionist theories. His verse becomes filled with that wondrous duality of transcendence and immanence which is the essence of Hebrew poetry, expressed with a poetic vigour which never conforms to any prescribed standards. His Tenth Muse never came into being, yet though his poetry is pervaded by ancient lyrical overtones, it is ever new and astonishingly moving.

Yitzhak Lamdan, too, came under the influence of European expressionism, but he very soon repressed his leanings to individualism and subjectivism, discarding them for a national 'lyrical self' that was charged with the three-fold task of Nation, Land and Language, the three attributes of Israel's re-demption. Of this individual self, this muse-inspired self, which he discarded, he writes in 'Ballad to my Other Self':

> A wheel of change revolving on its restless axis,
>   For which his eyes will always yearn.
> When all is clear, he tears away to mystery
>   Sailing from discovery towards a hidden shore.

Lamdan loved that 'other self', from which his national consciousness had obliged him to part, for once this had been 'the only self'. He devoted the full force of his expression to his people, whose redemption is no longer a destiny that is 'hidden' and 'occult'. For beyond this 'hidden and occult' lies the destiny of the Jewish people. His poem *Massadah,* which in its day stirred the hearts of the young who yearned for redemption, is a song of light, of the romance of light, the great shining light of the Land of Israel, symbolic of the ultimate heroic battle of those who died in the cause of freedom, and it is this light which must needs dispel the mists beyond which Israel's destiny lies hidden.

Lamdan re-sang his *Massadah* in numerous variations and also in ballad form—for the ballad speaks of man's meeting with his fate—using various biblical epics as his themes. One of these ballads is *'Jonah Fleeing from His God':*

> Thou hast found me, O Lord.
> Thy storm has caught me midst sea and sky.
> I said: 'Here a man may rest in the hold of the ship!'
> But not if he be the son of Amittai, wearied from truth-seeking.
> Only a man free from the yoke may rest,
> A man not bearing the double burden of nation and mankind
> As he gazes at the unchanging orbits of the stars.

Jonah seeks to rest from bearing the burden of destiny and prophecy. He no longer wishes to act as intermediary between God and man, between heaven and earth. All he wishes is to be like all other men, a member of a nation like all other nations, without any destiny to fulfil...

All Lamdan's poetry nevertheless conveys an ardent longing for the happiness that comes from the fulfilment of destiny; it is permeated with some secret hope that *Massadah,* rebuilt on firm foundations of rock and soil under the glare of a sun that dispels all 'shadow', will once again be an intermediary point between earth and heaven. For it is the tragedy of the nation, as well as the personal tragedy of the poet, that even after he has discarded 'that other self', he continues to yearn for it passionately; and just as the poetic muse has not been entirely extirpated from the sense of destiny which his poems convey, neither can it diminish the zeal of longing for this destiny, for both are closely interwoven.

This inner turbulence which overwhelmed both Uri Zvi Greenberg and Yitzhak Lamdan, fermenting the expressionist and national elements in their poetry into one spiritual symbiosis, was also characteristic of Avraham Shlonsky. He is commonly considered to be the father of modern Hebrew poetry. Yet every father is also a son, whose distinctiveness lies in the fact of his having rebelled against his own fathers, with whose heritage he ultimately becomes imbued. Shlonsky imbibed the works and spirit of Bialik and Tchernikhovsky, as well as the Futurist and Symbolist trends of Europe, but ultimately he was unable to escape the necessity of associating his poetry with some human, social and national object and of integrating himself into a world that imposed tasks and missions.

He rebelled against Bialik, but it was from Bialik that he learnt to acquire that vibrancy of language which restored to it its primal imagery and music. It was from Bialik, too, that he learnt to impart to words magical undertones of meaning and scintillating allusions. Ostensibly, he assumed the burden of poetry alone; but whoever assumes the burden of poetry, inevitably takes upon himself all other tasks, for poetry extends to all subjects, needs and aspirations. So long as things are merely said, they are not binding. And if they are binding upon the nation or the society, they still do not place any obligation on the individual, who is not tied to them by the bond of poetry. And if they are binding by virtue of their logic and reason, they are not necessarily binding on the soul, for they have not the kinship with the soul that poetry has.

The revolution of Israel has been very different from all other revolutions.

Whereas other revolutions set out to tear down what has been established and to uproot what has been planted, the revolution of Israel has aimed at *striking roots*. The revolution in Hebrew Poetry, likewise, has been a process of taking root, of embedding the language in the soil of its poetry, so that it may later blossom forth to convey the most complex emotive experiences—such as the imagery of Natan Alterman. It has meant implanting the creative language in a congenial soil, so that in hours of longing it may give forth the most subtle, fragrant refinements—as in the hyperbolic poetry of Leah Goldberg, which soars upward in a sweeping arc and returns to enrich this selfsame soil. This taking root, in all its variations, must needs invoke poetry where the element of Eros, too, is in evidence, where the savour of sensuality remains ever new and fresh and wondrous as in the myth; for, in the words of T. S. Eliot, 'Poetry is a personal myth.'

Shlonsky's poetry has all the immanence, experience and remembrance of the myth. What man has forgotten, his flesh still recalls:

> Our body remembers,
> Breathing the air of the ancient past.

Just as the myth, in its day, would create for man a pattern of the world and lend significance to all things, so poetry moulds life in a certain pattern and lends significance to man's will and desires. The whole world is the substance of Shlonsky's poetry, demanding that it be fashioned into a distinctive mould. Even creeds and outlooks and ideas are merely shapeless material, clay awaiting the trowel. After all his Aestheticist, Futuristic and Symbolistic divarications, the poet reverts to world-building poetry. His is a constructive revolution; for all evolution is but chaos if man does not direct it into poetic channels:

> Lord of the Universe! Builder of the Universe!
> Who measured out the world with plumb-line and compass
> Thou hast taught us to think and to speak.
> Guard us from garrulity and flowery speech.
> From garnering words to their ruin,
> From excessive, convulsive lamentation.
> Place a measure in our Jobian hand
> A builder's rule wherewith to conquer chaos.
> Teach us precision and accuracy in our words.
> Simplify the simple, the obvious, the constructed.

Natan Alterman is the most outstanding modern Hebrew poet of the Shlonsky school. His imagery is forthright, admitting of no interpretation, for any interpretation you might wish to impose on it would force you to render his poetry in unpoetic terms, severed from its linguistic roots and cut off from its very soul. His imagery admits of no interpretations, since it conveys a direct image of a world created by sight and sound. When the live-dead man ('a poor man is as good as dead', runs the saying) says to his wife:

For I swore—and you are my witness—
That you stand firmly on life.
By a lie they tore you from me
And in truth to you must I return.

you feel that you wish to extract the implication of these words and retain the distillation in your heart. But any interpretive prosaic 'intervention' distorts their poetic truth, rendering truth false, and falsehood true; for any distortion of the poetic pattern demolishes its essential truth.

The forthrightness of Alterman's poetry is an intensification of life and of the world. It employs a forceful, rhythmic movement that spans great distances. Just as motion and speed may change the mass and dimensions of material bodies, similarly verbal rhythms may alter the spiritual dimensions of language. Alterman's poetry defies any scientific conceptual definition. It strives to restore things to their pristine, aesthetic purity. It sends new blood coursing through words and re-awakens their dormant force, their power to effect that 'meeting without end' between man and the world, a meeting that is 'sudden and for ever'. The words thus become synaesthetic, endowed with a smile of true wisdom—that wisdom which can be found in poetry alone.

* *
*

This anthology includes works of Hebrew poets from Bialik to Meltzer. The next collection, now in preparation, will be representative of the younger generation of poets.

Translated by Joseph Shachter

CHAIM NACHMAN BIALIK

1873—1934

The greatest Hebrew poet of modern times. Born of poor parents in the
Ukrainian village of Radi and orphaned of his father at the age of seven,
he was given a strict religious upbringing by his grandfather. At fifteen
he went to study at the Volozhin yeshiva, where he remained for a year and
a half. Deeply influenced by the articles of Ahad Ha-Am, he was attracted
to the Haskalah and national revival movement. He went to Odessa in 1891
and moved in Jewish literary circles. He married at twenty and worked for
some years as a book-keeper in his father-in-law's timber business. From 1896-
1900, he taught in the Polish town of Sosnowice, later returning to Odessa
where he engaged in teaching and publishing and was for six years literary
editor of the weekly Ha-Shiloah. In 1921 he left Russia for Berlin, where he
founded the Dvir publishing house, later transferred to Tel-Aviv. He himself
settled in Tel-Aviv in 1924, devoting himself to cultural activities and public
affairs.

His poetry may be classified into verse expressing the national revival,
personal poetry, and songs of nature. His national poetry laments the de-
generation of the Jewish nation in the Diaspora and the decline of its
ancient culture; its inherent reproof is designed to stimulate the nation's
latent forces to arise and carve out a new destiny. This poetry is also bitterly
critical of the egoism and pettiness pervading Jewish society and the absence
of Jewish pride and human dignity at the nation's crucial hour. The most
important of these poems are Be-Ir ha-Haregah ('In the City of Slaughter'),
Achen Hatzir ha-Am ('Surely the People is as Grass') and Davar
('Word').

His personal poems express a variety of emotions: a lament for a life
that has passed without affording any inner satisfaction; man's transience
set against the eternity of the universe; the conflict between man's desire for
personal happiness and his sense of duty to his people—Megillat ha-Esh
('The Scroll of Fire'); man torn between his love for the old, established
world and his revolt against all that is decadent in it.

His songs of nature—Ha-Berechah ('The Pool'), Zohar ('Brilliance'),
Mi-Shirei Horef ('Of Winter Songs')—are rich in imagery and total expression. His love poems—Ayech ('Where Art Thou'), Tziporet ('The

Humming Bird'), Hachnisini Tahat Kenafayich ('Spread Your Wing'), Ha-Enayim ha-Re'evot ('Those Hungry Eyes')—express tenderness and violent passion

His stories—Aryeh Ba'al ha-Guf ('Aryeh the Burly One'), Ha-Hatzotz-rah She-Nityabshah ('The Trumpet that Dried Up'), Me-Ahorey ha-Gader ('Behind the Fence')—deal realistically with subjects drawn from contemporary events. His copious legends and folk-tales indicate a fertile imagination and frequently a sense of humour—Va-Yehi ha-Yom ('And it Came to Pass'), Aggadat Shelosha ve-Arba ('Legend of the Three and the Four'), Shor Avus ve-Aruchat Yarak ('The Ox in the Stall and the Meal of Green Fodder'). In Saphiah ('Aftergrowth'), he lyrically depicts childhood scenes and memories.

As translator (Don Quixote, William Tell, The Dybbuk, Shakespeare, etc.) he set a Hebrew stamp on the material. He edited and published works of Hebrew mediaeval poets.

Bialik's works have appeared in numerous editions. His letters have been published in five volumes and his recorded speeches in two volumes. A large body of writing has been devoted to appraisal and criticism of his work. His poems have been translated into Russian (by Jabotinsky), English (Snowman), French (Kimche), German (Miller) and Polish (Dickman).

A three-volume monograph on Bialik has been written by P. Lachover, and a concordance of his works has been compiled. A bibliography of part of Bialik's published essays has been compiled by M. Ungerfeld.

Twilight Piece

Up rose the sun again, again the sun set.
I didn't see.
Day followed day followed day, but not one note
From the sky for me.

Upon the western rim, the piled-up clouds again,
Hulk on hulk,   blazed.
Sages—what worlds are rising there?
What worlds being razed?

No worlds are rising there; no worlds are razed.
I only see
Imbecile evening scattering ashes on
The earth and sea.

'I looked for your penny, but I lost my crown'
Is what I see within;
While Mephistopheles behind me stands
Grinning his cruel grin.

Translated by Robert Friend

Midnight Prayer

A night of rain. A heavy wind drives
Dense clouds over the town,
That in its miry, restless sleep
Lies huddling down.

Dark entrances lie silent,
Only pounding rain falls.
The shivering, abandoned houses
Blacken their front walls.

Like orphans who are left alone
With no warm shelter from the kind,
Rafters draw themselves in close,
Shivering, softly whine.

As though they're churning evil thoughts
Muttering below their breath.
Curses for what holds them there,
Wishing its death?

The rain comes pouring, battering down
On the walls like great tears;
Roofs tremble and keep shuddering,
The town weeps its fears.

And those who sleep in darkness curse
In dreams tomorrow, yesterday.
Sleep easy, poor and beggared folk,
Dream peacefully.

Wind goes howling through the cracks,
Blood freezes at its sound.
Maybe it's some innocent cursing,
Whose life is draining down.

There's not one star left up on high;
No chink of light breaks there.
One lonely window-sill's lit up, where a Jew
Rises to his midnight prayer.

Translated by A. C. Jacobs

Morning Watch

Have you watched for the morning and seen the sure
Radiance of dawn stepping o'er the horizon?
Those bright rays of splendour, so brilliant, so pure,
Bursting in haloes, flashing wide, dashing high,
Till day is quite nigh
And the sun rises into the heaven—

How awesome, how luminous, this dazzling sight!
And as before the unveiling of a great holy secret
Your heart fills with wonder—but your mouth seeks the might
To draw it out of the heart, to give it a name
And render its flame—
But what tongue will know how to speak it?

Have you watched for the morning and seen the first sun
Of your people rise brilliantly skywards?
Rays in their thousands, on the chase, on the run
All bringing new lights, never stopping to rest,
Bursting east, bursting west,
Then thrusting now southwards, now northwards—

How exalted, how glorious, this marvellous sight!
How happy the eye that on watch spied a beam
And the mouth that gave praise to this heart-filling light,
And when dark clouds return us to wailing and woe,
Then that ray and that glow
In our tears will continue to gleam.

Translated by Richard Flantz

Pulse of Spring

There was a different spirit, the skies all ascended,
Bright distances appeared, broadening, extended—
The feet of spring stood on the mount!
Over the field at sunrise warm mists were bowing,
From the dew-covered trees tiny buds started growing—
There was a different spirit around.

The rays had not burst yet, no trumpets were ringing,
Of itself came the sound of pure simple singing,
Soft lights seemed to be emerging, arising, aspiring—
Not long now till they surge out, those forces long sealed,
Not long till the full strength of youth is revealed,
All those powers so great and inspiring.

And how sweet were the breezes, the spirit, the light,
Faces all smiling, and wherever your eyes might alight—
There was friendship beaming towards them.
And between one and all stretched threads made of gold:
Soon the white of the flowers would be unable to hold
This abundance of youth and its diadem.

Soon among those white flowers and rippling streams,
My new youth would have flowed, with my oldest of dreams
That the spirit of spring once had crowned.
And from my heart so full I'd have spoken each care,
And with glistening tears have cast out my despair—
There was a different spirit around!

Translated by Richard Flantz

Only a Single Ray

Only a single ray, but suddenly
You rise to glory and are half-divine;
one ray of sun unfolds the lure in thee,
unfolds the flesh. You ripen like a vine.

Only the tempest of a single night,
but it has ravished you of the sun's powers.
Already from afar, lewd dogs sniff out
the rotting corpse within the reek of flowers.

Translated by Robert Friend

Not by Chance

The light did not come to me just by chance,
And from my father I did not inherit it:
No, I scratched it out of my rock and my stone
And hewed it out of my heart.

A single spark hides in the rock of my heart,
A tiny spark, but all of it mine,
Borrowed from no-one nor stolen,
From out of me, always mine.

And from the hammer-blows of my sorrows,
When my heart, my rock, almost burst,
The spark took wing, sprayed into my eyes,
And from my eyes—to my verse.

And from my verse it will flee to your hearts,
And in your flame that I lit will fly higher,
And I, with my body and blood,
Will pay the price of the fire.

Translated by Richard Flantz

Alone

The wind took them,   light swept them all away,
The morning of their lives sang with a new sense,
I,   a soft fledgling,   remained below
The wing of God's presence.

I was left utterly alone,   and the Presence
Fluttered above my head her smashed right wing.
My heart knew her heart,   she trembled on
Her son,   her only one.

She was driven away from everywhere.
Only one small grim lonely place was left:
The house of study where she hid in shadow
And I shared her grief.

When my heart yearned for the window,   for the light,
When I grew embittered at her wing's hard weight
She laid her head on my shoulder,   her tears dripped
On the pages of the Talmud.

She wept to me softly and clung to me
As though I was enclosed by her smashed wing,
'The wind took them,   all grew and blossomed,
I stayed alone.'

And like the closing of a very old lament,
Like a prayer moving in pleading and in fear
My ear listened to that gentle weeping,
And to that scalding tear...

Translated by A. C. Jacobs

On the Slaughter

Crave pity for me, sky,
If you hold a God, and ways to him
That I have not found.
Say prayers for me.
My heart is dead: no prayer comes to my lips.
My hand is useless: there is no more hope.
For how long... till when... when?

Here's my neck, hangman—kill!
With your axe slice it like a dog's.
The whole earth's my scaffold.
There are not many of us,
And our blood's free—squirt out the murder blood!
It plays like a child and grows old on your shirt
And dries in for ever.

If there's any justice let it shine now.
But if it shines in the sky after I'm killed
Let its throne be smashed.
Let the sky lie festered with perpetual guilt,
And you proud ones walk in the violence
You begot and suckled.

Curse those who say, 'Vengeance.'
The Devil's not yet formed such vengeance
For the blood of a small child;
Its blood goes seeping through the abyss,

Seeps through the darkest parts,
Feeds in the darkness, and eats away at
All the earth's rotting supports.

Translated by A. C. Jacobs

After My Death

After I am dead
Say this at my funeral:

There was a man who exists no more.

That man died before his time
And his life's song was broken off halfway.
O, he had one more poem
And that poem has been lost
For ever.

He had a lyre,
And a vital, quivering soul.
The poet in him spoke,
Gave it all his heart's secrets,
His hand struck all its chords.
But there was one secret he kept hidden
Though his fingers danced everywhere.
One string stayed mute
And is still soundless.

But alas! all its days
That string trembled,
Trembled softly, softly quivered
For the poem that would free her,

Yearned and thirsted, grieved and wept,
As though pining for someone expected
Who does not come,
And the more he delays, she whimpers
With a soft, fine sound,
But he does not come,

And the agony is very great,
There was a man and he exists no more.
His life's song was broken off halfway.
He had one more poem
And that poem is lost,
For ever.

Translated by A. C. Jacobs

Spread Your Wing

Spread your wing to be my shelter.
Be my mother, sister, all.
Let my head nest in your bosom
And my prayers that vainly call.

Bend at dusk, the hour of pity,
My sorrows will confess the truth:
Youth exists here, so they tell me.
Where's my youth?

I'll reveal another secret:
My soul burnt itself alive:
Love exists here, so they tell me.
What is love?

There were stars, and they betrayed me.
There's no dream: there was before.
I have nothing left now, nothing,
Nothing more.

Spread your wing to be my shelter.
Be my mother, sister, all.
Let my head nest in your bosom
And my prayers that vainly call.

Translated by Dom Moraes

] 35 [

Prophet, Run Away

'Run away?'   I never run away.
I was taught to walk slowly by my flocks.
Glib words my tongue could never learn to say.
My words crash down as heavy as an axe.

I put forth all my strength and saw it fail.
Do not blame me: the guilt is yours: remember,
My hammer found   no anvil when it fell.
My axe went splintering through rotten timber.

So be it.   I, surrendered to my fate,
Tools knotted to my belt, turn in my tracks.
Like a day-labourer, unpaid and late,
On paths I came by I shall travel back.

I shall seek out the valleys of my home,
Make forest pacts with sycamores, and stay.
And you, to whom decay and plague have come—
Tomorrow's storm will flick you all away.

Translated by Dom Moraes

A Tendril Dropped

A tendril dropped to a fence and slept—
So I sleep too:
The fruit fell.   With my trunk and branches, what
Have I to do?

The fruit fell, and the flower is forgotten:
The leaves remain—
One day the storm will rise—they will be smitten
And drop down, slain.

The nights of terror will go on.   For me
No rest at all.
Lonely I thresh through darkness, hammering my
Head on the wall.

And once more spring will break, and only I
Shall hang upon
My trunk, a bald twig, whence all fruit and flower
And leaves have gone.

Translated by Dom Moraes

The Lengthening of the Days

FROM THE VISIONS OF THE LATTER PROPHETS

When the days, lengthening, grow like all the world's days,
All alike, all like yesterday and the yesterday before it,
Just days, lacking much pleasure and laden with sorrows,
Lashing animal and man with waste and with boredom,
And a man goes out to the seashore at sunset, to walk,
And sees that the sea does not divide,
And he yawns,
And he goes to the Jordan, and it does not recede,
And he yawns,
And he sees wise men and fools,
None budging from their places,
And he yawns,
And the man and the animal sit in boredom together,
The burden of their lives heavy upon them,
And each plucks the hair from his head in distraction
And the cat grows bald round the mouth.

Then the longings rise.
Of themselves they rise, like mushrooms raising a stench
In a plank of decaying wood:
The longings fill all the crevices and cracks,
Like rags filled with lice.
Then the man returns to his tent for supper
And dips crust and salt-herring in vinegar
And he longs;
He drinks up his cup of murky lukewarmness,
And he longs;

He strips off his shoes and jacket on the bedside
And he longs.
And the man and the animal sit in longing together,
And each wails in his dream from the vastness of longing
And on the tin roof the cat howls and scratches.

Then the hunger comes,
Exalted and wondrous, like nothing before it:
Not hunger for bread or for vision, but for the Messiah!

And early in the morning, with the sun not quite showing,
The man, exhausted from wandering, sated with dreams
And empty of soul,
The webs of an angry sleep still on his eyelids,
The dread of the night still twisting his bones,
Rises from his bed, from his tent's dark fastness
And, with the cat still wailing, its grating nails
Still scratching his brain and his entrails,
He hurries to his window and wipes off the scum
Or goes to his tent-flap and shades his eyes with his hand
And raises a blurred eye that is feverish and hungry for salvation
Towards the tiny path behind his paddock,
Towards the pile of rubbish opposite his house,
And seeks the Messiah!
And the woman wakes under the blanket and rolls over,
Wild-haired, flaccid of flesh and murky of spirit,
And, snatching her shrunken breast from her baby's lips,
She leans to one side and listens attentively:
Isn't the Messiah coming?
Has no-one heard his ass whinny?
And the baby in the cradle raises its head,
And the mouse peeps out of its hole:

Isn't the Messiah coming?
Has no-one heard the clinking bell of his ass?
And the maid heating water over the stove
Moves her soot-covered face and looks out:
Isn't the Messiah coming?
Has no-one heard the sound of his horn?

Translated by A. C. Jacobs

May I be One of You

May I be one of you, the silent of soul, the humble,
who weave your lives unseen, modest in thought and action;
hidden dreamers, sparing in speech, but augmenting the glory.
Within you, your spirit's beauty hides like a pearl in the sea depths,
and your virtues, like forest berries, increase in the dark of the shadows.
Your hearts are a sacred temple, and your closed lips are its portals;
nobles you are—unknown, and noble of spirit—unknowing,
poets of beautiful silence, priests of the stillness of God.
No eye of a stranger beholds the fêtes of your soul and its mourning;
there is always a light in your eye, of serenity and of sadness,
and always a smile on your lips, of wisdom and of forgiveness;
you welcome without judging whatever your path encounters:
the low as well as the high, the sin as well as the virtue.
Slow, slow, as if on tiptoe, you go along life's pathway,
heart wakeful, ear alert, your eye forever seeking,
soul open to every rustle, to every quiver of splendour,
carelessly sowing about you, without premeditation,
the faith and the purity that emanate from your being
as the blue flows from the sky and the shadows fall in the forest.

Well-learned you are in silence, and your voice and word are an
    absence;
your hand creates no greatness, your mouth will not speak greatly,
your desires expire in your heart and your longings die in your bosom;
you fight in no battle of seers; leave nothing for museums to inherit;
lonely your footsteps die, without an imprint or echo.
But your lives are your revelation; your very being—your glory.
God's image in the world has you for faithful preservers!

Daily, fragment by fragment, in the light of your eye, in your features,
your lives' beauty fills the world's hollows, as into the heart of a river
an underground spring will flow, reviving it unknowing.
Nothing, by God, will be lost; not one flutter of your eyelid,
not your soul's least tremor!
Like the song of stars, they will shimmer in the void of the
   world forever.
At the end of time when the echoes of Heman's songs have vanished
and all memory of the wisdom of Calcol and of Dara,
they will live again in the features, in the light of the eye of some man.

Translated by Robert Friend

Imperceptibly, One by One

Imperceptibly, one by one, like stars in the early morning,
my hidden desires go out, my grief ends silently,
but the last still hides within me, the howling of all my life.
Not day-murmur will silence nor any devil destroy it:
the desire to find once again before my days are over
—whether awake or in dream, no matter if once only—
grace in the eyes of God. Yes, let it come but once
—what if for one short minute—the vision of my dear childhood,
the morning of my life in the fullness of its first sweetness.

Corruption eats at my life, my own hands sully my crown,
I have forgotten the paths to my God, the ways to the gates
     of His mercy,
my ears are shut to His call, and my eyes to His beckonings,
I have been cast out of His sky, denied the planets of light,
the flower of the field does not know me, the ear of corn does
     not greet me,
my visions have gone from me, my spirit has grown estranged.
Nevertheless, somewhere, in the lap, in the heart of the world,
there where nothing is destroyed, no footstep obliterated,
my childhood's sacred image keeps to this very day
—like the signet ring of God—its imperishable essence.
There beyond time's changes, unharmed and still untarnished,
it shines to me from its setting as the morning star shines from
     the heavens,
watching my ways from afar, counting my every footstep,
its eyelids trembling towards me, its gentle splendour above me.
Landscape of my beginnings, far fields of my childhood

and all that surrounds it; fountain of my spirit,
soil of my roots, beloved home of my thoughts and longings,
corner of the world I hold most dear, earth's best spot—
nothing is fresher to me than its grasses' greenness,
and nothing sweeter than the blueness of its skies.
Its memory like good wine will never escape from the blood;
in my heart, forever white, live its first lucid snows—
dwelling place of my origins, my eyes' first landscape,
tranquil and solitary, modest in its fresh beauty,
decked with forests and mountains, and young in its earth and heavens,
sending its paths to the valleys, its trails to the golden corn,
silently stringing the days, the mornings and the evenings.
Wherever it exists on the face of the earth, this landscape
(with all its unfolding forms, in the freshness of its first splendour),
which the hidden finger of God has imprinted on my soul,
and which in my heart I shall carry to the world's last bourn, last day,
spring-soft or summer-bright, autumn-sad, or winter-cold,
exists in its innocence still, unchanged in the world around it,
silent when bright with the day or full of night's secrets,
watching over my pure breath, having my awe in its keeping
in the hollow of every stone, in the dimness of every corner,
in the trembling of driven leaves, the shadow of smallest clouds;
its woods are sentinels still, weaving a web of shadows,
not a single webbing is torn, not one twig missing,
still are their coverts filled with the sweet fears of my heart,
and my most tender dreams cast under one of their bushes.
Still as in my childhood stand the mountains there,
in their flower-woven carpets and sprinkled with the dew,
my steps are imprinted on them and still can be deciphered,
drenched are their valleys still with the glow of my first days,
in their crevices linger the cries of my soul's jubilation,
and voiceless my spirit there, still wanders wondering.

And my mother's poor dwelling, nest of my safety, tent of my peace,
abode of her joyousness, her sheltering shade and wing,
treasure-house of her fragrant kisses, fortress of her embraces—
it, too, wherever it is, somewhere in a far village,
atop its little hill, in the shade of a chestnut tree,
still keeps its ancient place and looks as it used to look:
small, white, and lovely—low-roofed and windows tiny,
moss padding its walls, grass peeping from its crannies,
wreathed with gardens and lots that are wildly overgrown;
with the caravans of cloud the years flow before it,
where it sits on its little hill, sits day and night,
It watches the paths of the world and dreams of me from a distance,
for my sake its walls grow silent, it thinks of me always,
my memory fills its recesses, my life's shadow haunts its rafters.

Only once, I know, does a man drink from the golden goblet,
the bright, the splendid vision is never granted twice;
for the sky with its azure look and the grass with its vivid greenness,
a world suffused with light, and every creature of God
wearing a face of splendour, is granted the child alone,
whose eye beholds it once, and beholds it no more,
Nevertheless God keeps for the man that He deems faithful
an unexpected blessing. No eye can see its channels,
no seer can tell its time. Silently I await it,
I wait it night and day; like a violin with tuned strings,
my spirit is ready for it. I do not know where and when,
neither the way of its coming, nor what angel will bring it to me.
One thing my heart tells me, one thing my soul know well:
I shall be granted the vision, I shall have my dearest wish.
And all the scenes of my childhood, so many and so varied,
with everything that surrounds them, will silently flow through
   my soul,

will pave in the heavens above me, like the bright dreams of morning,
their paths of splendour. Suddenly, the distant will draw near,
voices long sleeping wake, and colours and odours forgotten
revive and live again. The vision will last but a moment
but drenched by its sweet waves, I shall drain in that one moment
the nectar of my life in one enormous draught.
And once again I shall stand
breathless before a world miraculously pure,
a garden sealed and locked, strewn with riddles and wonders
no hand has violated, to which no lips have spoken;
heart overflowing, God's wonder in my face,
in my eye a sparkling tear, in my soul a dumb jubilation.

Translated by Robert Friend

Orphanhood

Strange was the way of my life—its paths were paths of wonder,
meeting between the gates of purity and defilement.
Holiness wallowed in blasphemy,   piety in the unholy.
There, in a human swine cave,   in the sacrilege of a tavern,
in fogs of incense, in steams   of impious libation,
behind the spiced-wine barrels,   over a yellow-leaved volume,
my father's head appeared,   the skull of a tortured martyr.
It floated over his shoulders   (as if beheaded) in smoke clouds,
His face sick with sorrow,   eyes shedding blood.
Silent between his knees,   I hung on his every word,
as the sots roistered about me,   as the drunks sprawled in their vomit.
The faces were monstrous,   depraved, the words a filthy stream;
hearing, the walls made grimaces,   the windows grew ashamed.
To a child's ear alone,   a child still innocent,
The murmur of pure lips   serenely, quietly flowed,
the murmur of Torah and Bible   and the words of the living God.

Not long did I see my father,   not long was my life with him.
When I was still young and tender,   unsated with his look,
when my eyes still called for his mercy,   my head for his sheltering
    hand,
death came and took him from me,   divided us forever;
but his image is deep in my heart: I call and he stands before me:
Like an exhausted ox   treading dumbly, slowly,
moving under its yoke,   wide-shouldered, heavy of step,
steady and stiff and restrained,   unchanged by time's changes
(dull days of sullen rain,   dog days of fevering wind),
treading in gloom and dragging   his life's crawling wagon

loaded with wearying stones   on roadways heavy with mud,
on pathways of shifting sand,   forever clouded with dust,
neck bent under the yoke,   brow furrowed with worry,
eyes deep wells of grief,   blankly, hopelessly staring
at every crossing of pathways,   at every meeting of roads:
Will there come from wherever he comes   a merciful one, a redeemer?
So have I always seen him   (and my soul grew dejected)
—torn from God's lap in the morning,   from the fountain of his life,
having doffed his garments of holiness,   removed his *tefillin* and
   prayer-shawl,
when his eyes still beheld the soul,   heart sang like a harp of wonder,
and his ears still heard the stars,   still heard their distant murmur—
go out submissive and quite   like a somnambulist
to the suffering of his days   and the sorrow of his hands:
He would sit his scorpion's day   among stretched-out revellers,
drinking the steam of their mouths,   defiled by the breath from
   their lips,
mounting the scaffold each day,   thrown to the lions each day.
And when he returned in the evening,   sweating with his disgrace,
drenched to the soul with disgust,   as if from a pit of filth,
my heart for his suffering went out,   I was smitten by his dumb grief.
If I had not been so young,   if I had not been so weak,
I'd have put my neck to his neck,   my shoulder to his shoulder,
bearing his burden with me,   the yoke of his suffering.
If we had shared the burden,   he might have found it lighter.
But wish exceeded reach,   my prayers were all still-born.
He went his way as always,   his lonely way of troubles,
soul bent to the ground with the burden and the effort,
and when they grew too much,   his heart broke and he died.
In the middle of his days   he fell down suddenly,
fell like a felled ox,   down in the roadway
and never rose again.

At the far end of the graveyard,
behind the slum of the tanners,   the dwelling place of the poor,
among the graves of his brothers,   the hungry, the poverty-stricken,
laid like himself in the soil   of death before their time,
washed clean of the dust of his world   and cleansed of the filth
    of his days,
in grave cloths white as his soul,   white as the snows of morning,
wrapped in a shabby prayer-shawl,   yellow as his books' pages,
pervaded like them with mercy,   pervaded like them with prayer,
kissed by trembling lips   and drenched with holy odours,
under a wooden grave mark   of boards thin and hollow,
on a day of Elul,   his bones at last found rest.
And over his head an inscription   carved by no artist's hand
in faith attests: '*Hic Jacet*   a simple, honest man.'

Translated by Robert Friend

Do not, although

Do not,
although he has exposed himself to you
   in utter nakedness,
bellow like bulls; he mocks you pitilessly
   and makes you pitiful.
You are too small for the meanings of his heart.
   He will reveal
not even the thousandth part
   of what he thinks of you—
baring himself the better to conceal
   himself, to vanish from your eyes,
lead you astray.
   In the covert of his poems you search for him
in vain. They, too, conceal his secrets. But
   between the verses, as between the bars
of a steel cage, a sly, a burning lion peers,
   seemingly calm, resigned, or growling quietly—
a roaring fire shut up in his bones.
   One night, in the midst of your sweet sleep,
from a distance that you cannot guess,
   from a howling wilderness,
suddenly you will hear
   the echo of its thunder in dismay.
You will not understand.
   But a cage will have been broken, a lock
shattered, the lion escaped to his home.
   And in the morning of that night, at rise of sun,

magnificent, strong-hearted, he will stand
   atop a rock,
burning in his golden curls, ringed by his mane,
   everything about him crying King.
His nostrils will scent the quarry; his eyes flame with scorn;
   his roar of freedom shiver the roots of the mountains.

Translated by Robert Friend

Neither Night Nor Day

When it's neither night nor day,
Secretly I'll make my way

To a place that's hard to reach,
The hovel of a crazy witch,

Who works in magic charms and spells,
Reads the future and foretells.

I will get her to tell me
Who my husband's going to be.

Where'll he come from, highland, lowland,
Lithuania or Poland?

Come riding grandly up our track
Or walk with a bundle on his back?

And what will be the gifts he brings,
Fine necklaces, or diamond rings?

What'll he look like? dark or fair?
Still single or a widower?

But Oh, suppose, dear witch, he's old—
I won't listen, won't be told.

If he's old I'll tell my father:
Shoot me, kill me I'd much rather.

I will fall and kiss his knees:
Not, not an old man, father, please.

Translated by A. C. Jacobs

SHAUL TCHERNIKHOVSKY

1875—1943

Poet and author. Born in Michaelovka, in the Crimea, he went to Odessa in 1890 to study at a school of commerce, and soon began publishing his first Hebrew poems. He later studied medicine at Heidelberg and Lausanne, graduating as a physician in 1907. Returning to Russia, he was imprisoned for three weeks as a political suspect. For three years he practised as a country doctor, then later in the towns of Grodno, Kiev and Petrograd, and served in the Russian medical corps in World War I. From 1922-31, he lived in Germany and thereafter in Palestine, where he worked as an attending physician at Tel-Aviv municipal schools.

His poetry comprises both national and universal elements. In his early verse he revolts against the moral and didactic motifs formerly characteristic of Hebrew poetry and calls for greater human freedom and free rein for man's natural impulses. His compositions are based on the expression of the emotions of love and joy of living and on a pantheistic attitude to nature. He seeks to bring out points of convergence between the ancient Judaic and Hellenic cultures. His idylls, depicting Jewish life against the setting of the Crimean townlet, are charged with a keen power of observation and plastic portrayal alongside philosophical reflections on man's place in the universe and on the eternal and the transitory, the whole being pervaded by a wholesome humour and sense of joie de vivre. *Embracing a wealth of various forms, his poetry is charged with a sense of the primal function of art in human society. His major poetic work* Ama de-Dahavah *('The Golden People') contains philosophical reflections on the life of the bees and the life of man.*

In addition to poetry, he wrote the drama 'Bar Cochba', stories, essays and a monograph on Emanuel the Roman, the Hebrew poet.

His collected works (including translations) have been published in ten volumes, and his poems, collected into one volume, have been published in numerous editions.

A prolific translator, his translations into Hebrew include Homer's Iliad *and* Odyssey, *Sophocles'* Oedipus Rex, *the* Odes of Anacreon, *Plato's* Banquet, The Epic of Gilgamesh, *the Finnish epic,* Kalevala, The Lay of the Host of Igor, *Longfellow's* Hiawatha, *Shakespeare's* Twelfth Night, *Goethe's* Reynard the Fox *('Reineke Fuchs'), ancient Babylonian ballads and other works.*

Ballad of the King of Jeshurun

There was a King in Jeshurun
  And the captains gathered where
He stood with his sword and waited
  On a hillside high and bare.
There was a King in Jeshurun
  On a hillside high and bare.

There was a King in Jeshurun
  And many maids had he.
Busy hands at the spindle!
  And one with the soul of beauty.
There was a King in Jeshurun
  And one with the soul of beauty.

She kept no unguents ready.
  She did not bathe in myrrh.
Men coveted her body.
  Her eyes shed light round her.
She kept no unguents ready
  Her eyes shed light round her.

There was a king in Jeshurun.
  The Philistine camped round the hill.
He called his fighters to him
  And they went out to kill.
There was a King in Jeshurun
  And they went out to kill.

Going down he forgot it all—
  His wealth, and his fame that was
Bruited from pole to pole
  And the maids of his great house.
Going down he forgot it all—
  The maids of his great house.

A hawk soared: he did not stare.
  The grave before him lay.
He saw only the loved one there.
  He saw the lit eyes that day.
A hawk soared: he did not stare.
  He saw the lit eyes that day.

He would not come back alive
  By this path, he knew: it was fit:
For he had grown old in his love
  And so young he could die in it.
He would not come back alive
  So young he could die in it.

Translated by Dom Moraes

The Poem's Song will not Die

The poem's song will not die, the poem's song will never die.
The day the worm of man pours his dominion on all the world,
When over all the depths and heavens his mighty rule holds sway,
Harnessing lightning bolts and mastering the thunder's roar,
When over night's deep darkness falls the brilliant light of day;

And when evening falls in daytime from rising clouds of smoke,
And billows mass round chimneystacks turning blue skies into mires,
When, like nets the weary fisherman may from the water yoke,
The canopy of fog descends on a design of electric wires;

And when the winged warbler on a bush in a valley glade,
Falls suddenly to earth, for an arrow has struck it dumb,
And each tree of the eternal forests, that with the skies once played,
Falls kneeling to the axe, for its end too has come;

When gunpowder then vanquishes the summits of rocky heights,
And along the ridges of God's mountains its fiery path blasts by,
When the magic shade of evening banishes the radiant glow of lights,
And the tower pierces clouds, the column meets the sky,—
The poem's song will not die, the poem's song will never die.

Then in the whining of the cross-saw and the thunder of the hammer,
In the din of molten metal, where walls of foundries shake,
Wherever a man's heart beats: in village calm or city clamour
And in the sighs of love—the poem's song will wake.

And sending forth its voice over all of man's vast nation,
Through mines where men delve deep to the abyss beneath the sod,
With the fiery force of love, it will surge like the stormy ocean,
From a heart of pure belief, to the scenes and acts of God.

Filled with hues of gold, and wrapped about in rhymes,
The poet's thought will flow, like the pastures of the sea,
Recalling mighty forbears, and works of ancient times,
And the endless future joys of the people yet to be,—
The poem's song will not die, the poem's song will never die.

Translated by Richard Flantz

The Death of Tammuz

Come out and weep,
Daughters of Zion,
For Tammuz, fair Tammuz, the summer, is dead!
The coming days shall be days of cloud,
Days of souls' eclipse and of autumn unwanted...

With the first glint of sun
On this morning so bright
Let us out to the woods that are darker than night,
To the woods that are hidden in secrets and dreams,
To the dais of Tammuz, to the dais of light.

What dance shall we dance
All around the dais?
What dance shall we dance to Tammuz today?
We shall sway, we shall prance, to the right, to the left,
We shall kneel, we shall pray: 'Come back here to stay!'

We shall sway, we shall prance,
To the right, to the left,
Feet firm and straight, slowly hands touching hands,
Then out we shall go to seek Tammuz, the summer,
Boys and girls apart in two separate bands.

On the broadest of highways
We went looking for Tammuz—
Along avenues drenched in sunbeams and light,
So cheering to hearts in their warmth and their calm:
The thrush pauses there, and the pigeon in flight;

On a narrow path stretching
Between fields of tall grain,
Spread with poppies and thorns, each wild growing thing;
Beside bubbling springs among rustling reeds,
Where fresh rushes and canes sing sprightly of spring;

Then down to the brook,
Across hills and dales,
Past bushes and ruts and deeply-hoed furrows...
O wind frolicking in the grass, answer us!
Have you seen Tammuz, O pheasants, O sparrows?

We sought Tammuz...
Among autumn leaves,
In forests of pine, beneath treetops that swing,
Lest he sleep, drowsing in a cedar's shade,
To the scent of mushrooms joining his ring.

We sought Tammuz...
We found him not!
We climbed up the hills and down to the dells,
Tracking the traces of each hint and wonder,
Everywhere, in each place where God dwells.

We saw the tangle
And the trees of Astarte,
And the mysteries of the grove—all food for fire...
Only the crying of hungry-bellied fledglings
Around the dais; the dais a silken pyre.

And over cascades of streams
Where we said—
But spirits tell it in magical wording,
In a screech and a scream to the reeds that dried
To their roots in the heat, that summer's returning.

No traces were found
Of demons in pastures,
And the sound of their laughter ceased with their secrets few;
Cattle graze on the pasture, and goats dance
Around the waterholes on mornings drenched with dew.

Come out and weep,
Daughters of Zion,
See the world's sorrow, without miracle outspread,
The world's sorrow, in its soul's eclipses:
For bright Tammuz is gone, for Tammuz is dead.

Translated by Richard Flantz

To the Sun

[I]

I was to my god like a hyacinth, or a violet,
   Like a bright sheaf of gold in the heavy wild corn;
   And he brought me warm mists on a cold mountain morn,
Symphonies of light and shade, blue, calm and scarlet.

I grasped the time's sorrow, heard the songs men create—
   Voices shedding light, in alien darkness crying:
   Between the living and those already dying,
Had I come too early or was my creator late?

Still in my heart sleeps dew that falls on Edom's sod,
High on the holy mount, home of the primal god,
   For my heart murmurs songs to sun and Orion.

When pods burst, fruit ripen, and leaves of saplings sprout,
A dead world's idols grab me, and there's no way out—
   Or a last statue from the age of the lion?

Translated by Richard Flantz

To the Sun

[II]

Hyacinth and mallow was I to God: lifelong
Only this pure sun fills, for each, the earth,
And an angel urges: 'Bud, child, and bring forth
Among the biting thorns, your festive song'.

The damp field suckled me: the smell, so near,
Of crumbled clods, rose to my head: did he
Not have a father and a priest in the city
That he fetched me to be his prophet here?

Shall the sap of the silver fir seem less in my eyes
Than your holy oil: gold on the head? There rise
Odours from pears and the fields that once I kept:

Are these less than the phials of Sheba where spikenard slept?
Slowly I bowed, honouring you without fear,
Like a golden stalk in the heavy-headed wheat.

As I stood between those who live and those who die
(Terrible craft!) a scalpel sharp in my hand,
Some wept for joy, and some swore at me, and
I drew the last light from the strange dying eye.

To the powerful thunder of cannon rolled over this place,
And the single light that in my deep tunnel glows,
I incised the last line, I rubbed out all those
Alive: so a jewel is torn from its onyx case.

But in that final spark of the dulling eye,
In the light which draws in all light, before the last,
In the feverish flash of that fire flying by,

In the fire which calls for fire and rules the host
Of terrors, you stood.   I was dazzled, you were so great.
Have I come too early, or did He make me too late?

Translated by Dom Moraes

from "Elka's Wedding"

MORDECHAI OF PODOVKA

Evening has fallen; the merchant,   Reb Mordechai of Podovka,
sits on the stoop of his house,   white in its new coat of plaster,
though hidden under the necklace   of the scarlet-peppers that
   hang there
drying in the sun—provisions,   with the gourds harp-shaped and
   golden,
for the fall days approaching. This   is the hour when shepherd
   and cowherd
return at last from the pastures   in a riot of din and confusion,
in clouds of flying dust.   To their calves mournfully bleating,
prevented by their owners   from browsing in the green pastures,
cows moo in answer: to come and suck their teats.
To the bleating of their lambs   ewes bleat in return.
Shrilly the wives of the farmers   call in their sheep and cattle,
cry them into the courtyard.   The sullenly barking dogs
help them round up the oxen,   the lambs and the silly sheep,
drive them to trough and barn   of these heroic wives.
Ears grow deaf with the din,   eyes fill with the dust and sand.
Mordechai sits on the stairs,   stickily sweating and tortured
with the heat of the sun and the tumult   that have ruled in his
   house since the day
of his only daughter's betrothal;   when the tailor, the butcher,
   the baker,
the cobbler and cobbler's apprentice,   began to visit daily;
when the stitchers of linens and frocks,   plain cooks and pastry cooks
and cooks to spoil the broth   (in Mordechai's colorful words)
turned masters in his house;   with the furniture taken away:

table and chair and stool,   and not excluding the bed;
and the couch expressly designed   for his afternoon siesta
became a dumping place   for shirts and blankets and sheets,
pillows, bed covers and shawls;   for blouses of every description,
the most expensive capes—   topped with hoods of fine lace,
or fringed with tassels of silk;   spilling over with day-cap and
   night-cap,
or modest or smartly immodest;   with smock and sock and stocking
and aprons meant for show,   with a sleeve peeping out here and there,
and hem and ruffle and train.   They overflowed the house,
and he took second place   to women's finery
and the latest wedding dresses.   He was dwindled, deprived of his
   honor,
and no one pays him heed.   In addition to all the 'hoo-ha,'
(which is hullaballoo in his language)   he has no rest—even now;
for right at this very moment   Meir the contractor is with him,
a smirksome, irksome bore,   who tortures the life out of people
because his words have no measure: he drags them out in a whine;
and Mordechai sits and sighs   because the stars have so written,
because it is so decreed   that he alone should be target
of the boring contractor's words.   And Mordechai, as his words
keep grinding on and on,   pretends to listen to him,
agreeing with curt Amens.   What was Mordechai like
at this strategic hour?   Like a low fence besieged,
which the enemy has surrounded   with a high siege-wall,
raising a rampart around it,   hurling catapults and arrows,
a shower of stones from slings.   Thus sat Mordechai
as Meir kept hurling his words: seizure and sequestration;
summons and power of attorney;   purchase, collection of debts;
court mortgage, accreditation;   bond and deed of assessment;
defence attorney, reversion;   tenure, freehold and fee-simple;
chattels, movables, traps;   appeal and counter-appeal;

waiver, complaint, and so on.   Mordechai shrinks in his bones;
and Meir keeps casting his stones.

Who knows how all would have ended   were it not (it was none
    of his doing)
that relief came to Mordechai.   He was consulting his kidneys:
What should he do to Meir?   Stand firm and send to the devil
his father and mother and sons   to the last of their generations?
Or simply ask him sweetly: Have you said your evening prayers?
But here comes Mordechai's daughter,   Elka, the modest bride,
and with her comes Aunt Frieda…and interrupt the talk…
'What is my pigeon doing?   Is this a time to be gadding
when your mother can hardly breathe   and her poor feet are swollen
with all her running about   making the needed arrangements?'
'Please!' Aunt Frieda replied.   Meir shut up like a clam,
choking on one of his stones.   'We've been to the cemetery
to invite our Auntie Ettel   and our little sister Perel
to the wedding that will take place   if the good God wills it so.
Have we done something wrong?   That used to be the custom,
brother. And if they know,   they'll certainly be happy
with Elka's happiness.   Surely there in heaven
their merit will defend us   and lead to our redemption.'
Mordechai knows too well   Aunt Frieda has a tongue
and whenever she opens her mouth,   the old familiar grinder
grinds the same coffee beans: erodes the mountains and skies,
raves about trees and stones,   foresees to the last generation,
and ends—with a handful of beans.   From the frying pan into the fire,
but to forestall the disease   he has the remedy.
'Dear sister, of course. How right   that you didn't forget the dead.
Of course you had to invite them.   Blessed is he who reminds us
of that which is forgotten.   Tonight, just after supper
we'll read the list together   of those (may the good God spare them)

of the living we have invited,   to see that we haven't confused
natural or social boundaries,   or left somebody out.
That would make people angry;   such anger and disgrace
would never be forgiven.   Meir, get a move on.
We're late for evening prayers.'

                                        After supper they sat
all three of them together: Mordechai, Elka, Aunt Frieda,
but not his wife Chi-ena,   because that efficient woman,
was deep in her own affairs—   head spinning like a wheel.
They sat in the open passage   around a table, and Mordechai,
his glasses on his nose   and guest list in his hand,
called out name after name   and ticked them as he read.
Mordechai read and ticked,   and they listened as they sewed.
The village A-hymani—   there are two listed here:
Haletsky and old Lisovsky,   friends from the good old days—
they'll certainly come to the wedding.   Kaminka (on the shores
    of the Konka,
which flows into the Dnieper),   a village the pious founded
who once were of Dohbrooja,   lovers of kitchen gardens,
with much corn in their barns—   another two: Litvinsky,
the greatest clown in the world,   my cousin at third remove;
and that pedant Tsirlin—   they'll certainly come to the wedding.
The inhabitants of Tawmock,   famed for its plaster and thieves—
they'll have it in for me   if my note doesn't reach my friends there:
old Kaharlitsky and Snitzer.   They'll certainly come to the wedding.
And Vinetsky of Laypehsicha,   (that large and prosperous village
full of all good things)   will take leave of his business,
for we went to school together!   A true, whole-hearted friend—
he'll certainly come to the wedding.   And here's huge Mihailovka,
heavy with its good wheat,   and famed for a large population.
Now listen carefully: Kornblitt and his five sons—

'the ten sons of Haman';   Piatigorsky who deals in flour,
a tax collector for ages;   Gordin, skilled in skullduggery;
Yonni, his son;   Slavintonter;   Serebrennick who lends out money
at a steep rate of interest—   all old friends of mine.
They'll certainly come to the wedding.   And from the village Skelky,
excelling in honey and wax,   these three: Chmelnitsky and Brin
and my dear old Auntie Yentel,   real and perfect friends.
They'll certainly come to the wedding.   I list from Upper Rogachik,
a town of miserable potters: Tsiparsky, Dov Lebedinsky,
and Rafael Chotinsky—   all distant relatives.
They'll certainly come to the wedding.   Yantsikrak: Chatsirevich,
nicknamed Scare-Crow-revich,   dearer than a brother—
he'll certainly come to the wedding.   The village Bilizirki,
which the Jews call Little Gypsy: two of the Bohuslavskys,
Lihovitzer, the swindler—   all dear friends of mine.
They'll certainly come to the wedding.
From Seregozi, Litvinsky;   from Mentsikuris, Litrovnik,
Zalman the jolly beggar,   Vengerov, professional sage.
Blood-brothers, allies, friends—   they'll certainly come to the
    wedding.
And here from big Kachoovka,   which is famous for its market:
the half-hearted heretic Karp   and the rough old man Olaynov—
both dear to me, good friends.   They'll certainly come to the
    wedding.

Thus did he sit and explain,   write, rub out, and write
as the silent and fragrant night   peeped through window and door,
and the sects collected for worship,   the little disciples of God:
mosquito, locust and moth,   and the butterfly of night
that now began to dance   around lamp and candle flame.

Translated by Robert Friend

The Bells

Through the roaring of bells—to blood calls the song.
Ding-Dong! Ding-Dong! Ding-Dong!
The city is fallen! The mob's attacks
Sweep the people to slaughter—their wrong
And shame all swathed in sacks.

Two days the rolling heaps of corpses filled the town;
On the third they were flung in the pit;
And then the temple was befouled (with dung of swine thrown down
To smear all the Scrolls of Holy Writ.)
Then they raised there a tower white and strong,
And in it a bevy of bells,
And when the priest would arise to bless the throng,
Their reply came in swells:
Ding-Dong! Ding-Dong!

To one of the Just the story was blown,
And he came there one night, in autumn, alone,
To recite the sacred 'Kaddish':
'Yisgadal veyiskadash...'
And it came to pass when he ended—and no man
There with him, naught but the slumbering night—
That the gong resounded in the tower so white,
And all the tiny bells responded again:
'Amen
'Amen! Amen!'

The priest hurried there on hearing this song,
The multitudes came and gathered in thrall,
Hegemons, archhegemons, bishops and all;
They poured holy water and sang loud and long
To mend the bells in the tower so tall,
And from up above came the reply of the gong,
Of the tiny bells too
With glorious ado:
'Ding-Dong! Ding-Dong!'

But at midnight service of the Jews that night,
The sign was given again:
Once more the gong sighed in the tower so white,
And the tiny bells sighed in refrain,
In a ringing of beauty, in a ringing of pain:
'Amen!
'Amen! Amen!'

Translated by Richard Flantz

With this Ring I Thee Charm

With this ring I thee charm in the rite
Of the butterfly born to its world,
To its life of one day, the bridal night
Of one hour amid coloured wings.
With this ring I thee charm in the plight
Of choirs of mosquitoes that dance
In the forest clearing, in the light
Of their mute song of noon's fiery romance.

With this ring I thee charm in the rite
Of the rustling tree and the plants
Fluttering in the breeze, that recite
In the tongue of aromas and speak only scents.
With this ring I thee charm in the ways
Of that great yearning that sings,
The great yearning, so silent always,
That blossoms again every year, every spring.

With this ring I thee charm in the rite
Of the bellowing deer that broods
In longing for a mate, at twilight,
With glowing horns at the edge of the woods.
With this ring I thee charm with the power
Of all the might in animal essence,
Of worlds once destroyed and reborn in the roar
Of all the thousands of tribes of existence.

With this ring I thee charm, in the deep
Secret of all the poems of man and his song,
Of his magician's words, of the glories that sleep
In the mysteries of his faith, hidden so long
In the guess and the stress of each human heart,
In the source of his dance and the base of his art.
Bewitched, now be still—and never depart—
I thee charm now forever... till death do us part...

Translated by Richard Flantz

The King

And he came to the hill. There he met
A company of prophets descending from the high place;
Before them one carried three kids,
And another a wine-skin and harp
And they gave him two kids, and two loaves,
And the wine-skin and the harp.—He took them.

And the Spirit of God came upon a prophet,
And one of them spoke, saying: 'Welcome,
Blessed among men, anointed of God,
Exalted over his brothers! Twice blessed
In the blessing of great sufferings and their joy
And in the joy of a lord of his brothers and master of his sorrows,
Girt in the mysteries of a ruler whose word
Decides for life or for death,
Who is drunk in great passion, that of a visionary
With eyes open to gaze on the shadow of the living God.
Even more exalted you, your heart shall be so pure
That it will absorb of the sublime light;
And if you are not holy, your soul shall hurt
From the touch of the wings of infinity, as they fleet
Through eternities pouring into eternities
To know the secret of final freedom...'

And he went up the hill and to the high place,
To the prophet of the living God,—the greatest
Of his brothers the prophets—glorious and grey.

And he carved the kid—and they roasted it,
And he blessed the bread—and they ate it,
And he tasted the meat—and they were sated.

And when they were sated one plucked upon the lyre,
And they all lifted up their voices in song.
And as they sang the spirit suddenly descended on them,
And each gripped the other's hand, right hand
In left and left hand in right,
And they lifted their feet and started to move
In a dance of devotion before the altar,
And they leaped and they pranced with all their might,
And the King also joined in the dance.

And hand in hand then the prophets pranced,
To the right, to the left, they backed and advanced,
Then leaping ahead, now swaying, now cheering,
As in siege of a wall, like besieged disappearing;
From moment to moment their joy gathered might,
As their bodies strained for the heights, for the height.

Then the King put aside his coronet of gold,
He cast away the ornament of splendour,
And the crown fell to the ground, where it bounced
And resounded and again rolled and rang.
Then also fell the dividing wall
That stood between him and all his people,
The division erected by man for man,
And he was as all Israel, one of his people.

And arm in arm then the prophets swirled,
To the right, to the left, they yelled and they whirled,
Splitting apart, returning, uniting,

In a circle of bustle, rearing and rioting;
From moment to moment their joy gathered might,
As their hearts yearned for the heights, for the height.

Then he put aside his cypress-wood harp,
He cast his instrument of song into the bushes,
And the harp fell among the tangle of branches,
Where its strings broke. Each string with its sigh.
Then also fell the dividing wall
That stood between him and all men,
The division erected by the Creator of the world,
And he was as all men on earth.
And hand in hand then the prophets went wild,
To the right, to the left, aloft now, in flight,
Embracing each other, and cleaving and cleaving,
Body to body, kissing and heaving;
From moment to moment their closeness gained might,
Their being would end in the heights, in the height.

Then he put aside his sword, the sword of his pride,
He cast his implement of war into the rocks,
And the weapon fell upon the stone,
Where it hit the rock, and rang out.
Then also fell the dividing wall
That stood between him and all life on earth,
The division of hate between life and man,
And he was as all that lives on the face of the earth.

And body to body the prophets whirled striving,
Straining to the skies but never arriving,
Straining in fury, to the right, to the left,

Between body and body no difference, no cleft;
From moment to moment their frenzy gained might,
As their souls longed for the heights, for the height.

And he put aside his clothes, the robe of his rule,
He cast his raiment of monarchy to earth,
And the cloth of his splendour fell on the path,
Where it lay gleaming, embroidered and white.
Then also fell the dividing wall
That stood between him and all of Creation,
Erected by the forces of *In the beginning,*
And he was as all that was wrought by God's word.

In one many-faced body the prophets united,
Leaping right, leaping left, dancing, excited,
Tripping on tree trunks and stray altar stones,
Rolling on grass and down scented lawns;
From moment to moment their union gained might,
As their spirits rose up to the heights, to the height.

And the Spirit of God came upon His anointed;
And the King began prophesying among them,
And became one with the universe and the fulness thereof,
One tiny spark in the infinity of being,
Loving and cleaving to all of Creation.
And he fell down naked, all that day,
And all the night...naked...naked...naked...

Translated by Richard Flantz

From Poems to Ilil

I will give her my songs, verse singing of the sea,
(Though they won't name her, or keep her name's memory)

Songs to the waves, to sand, to the crying sea-mew,
Small restless clouds, songs shaped without their clue,

And these songs still shall be hers alone
While my heart's strings tremble with her tone,

And I go wandering from sea to sea,
From snow in the north to desert sanded dry,

For her two eyes are two pale green seas
That hold my life and twine its mysteries.

Translated by A. C. Jacobs

The Dancers

Drum to drum speaks out and rends, drum to drum an order sends!
She to the drum, the drum to her—blade with hilt in union blends.
And all the girls now drum and dance—
Storms of wastelands, whorls of sands;
Before the assembled tribes in mischief they rise:
Wild... attuned... calves erect, with heavy thighs;
Whores in their holiness, impudent in their innocence—
Breasts that demand, calves that inflame the bridegroom's sense,
Dancing they hunt now, flaunting their charms,
Spells ringing from bracelets, demand tingling from arms—
'—Ho, brave bridegroom, to the tabernacle, sanctify!
Take my flesh, my cold breast, and make fire fly!
—My ankle no man has seen, my slim ankle, my bud—
I shall bare it, my hem, and thrust boiling through blood.
—Give me seed of a stiff-necked generation, a seed of bold bloom!
Impregnate me, lover of lovers, lover, husband and groom!
—And my seed shall be holy, the seed of passionate sleep,
With holiness of mystery, of desire painless and steep.
—Seed of a proud generation, angry-eyed like the desert, not
    knowing reprieve,
That will see signs and wonders—and will not believe!
—A generation worthy of its graves among deeps and sands
Over desert graves of pride mourned by voiceless bands.
—A generation worthy of its death, by the snakebite that mocks:
Snakes sent by gods, a generation of iron and rocks!'
They fly, their weaving sinews claiming the press of embrace,

Each crease of a robe, each beckoning calf making men's blood race;
Mothers of tribes, holy mothers of a nation,
Raising its hosts of thousands with powerful passion,
Sowing seeds of its future, of the last day's final gains,
A generation to stand in blood and fire, in deserts and plains,
Enough for swords of legions, for wheels and racks and pyres
And living graves... till each torturer and hangman tires;
Enough for maws of desert beasts, and to fall defending walls,
To sate the points of knives, to fill the deepest holes.

Before the assembled tribes in mischief they rise,
Mothers of a nation: calves erect, with heavy thighs.

Translated by Richard Flantz

Eagle, Eagle!

Eagle! Eagle on your hilltops, eagle flying o'er your hills!
Slow and buoyant—it seems a moment—only floating as it wills;
Floating, sailing through blue seas, hearing notes of sung delight
Filling heavens as it hovers, circling mute in burning light.

Eagle! Eagle on your hilltops, eagle flying o'er your hills!
Straight of back and heavy-bodied, broad of wing with blackest quills;
Flying tense (a speeding arrow), orbits spinning high and round,
Seeking traces of its quarry in dust and crannies on the ground.

Eagle! Eagle on your hilltops, eagle flying o'er your hills!
Fleeting, falling, sweeping wonder, wings not wavering as it spills:
For a moment freezing; then—the slightest motion of its wings,
Just a tremor, then of a sudden, up into a cloud it springs.

Eagle! Eagle on your hilltops, eagle flying o'er your hills!
Slow and buoyant—so it seems—a moment floats just as it wills...
Earth, the eagle's on your hilltops—o'er your surface casting shade,
With mighty wings it passes over, caressing hills that God has made...

Translated by Richard Flantz

] 83 [

You See, O Earth

You see, O earth, how very wasteful we have been:
In your secret laps of blessing we hid seed—not the clean
Glass-clear pearls of spelt, but seeds of heavy wheat,
Grains of yellowish barley, oats on frightened feet.

You see, O earth, how very wasteful we have been:
Flowers of flowers we hid in you, fresh with glorious sheen;
They were kissed by the earliest kiss of the sun just coming up,
Burying beauty with graceful stem, with the crown of the willing cup;
Before they could know noon in the midst of innocent sorrow,
Before dreaming of light in growth or drinking dew upon the morrow.

The best of our sons we brought you, youth of purest dreams,
Clean in heart and deed, untouched by earth's dark streams,
The cloth of their years yet woof, a cloth of hopes to be,
We have none better than these. Earth, did you see?

And you shall cover them all. Let the plant rise in its season!
A hundred gates of might and glory, for people, homeland vision!
They atone for our lives in glory, their sacrifice unseen…
You see, O earth, how very wasteful we have been.

Translated by Richard Flantz

Three Donkeys

Three donkeys from Beersheba, so they say,
Plodded slowly down the road to Dan one day.
One brown, one black, one white, they went their way.

The three passed by a minaret, and there
The black one crouched, hearing the call to prayer.
The three passed by a monastery in line
And there the brown one knelt before the shrine.
The three passed by a holy ruin: it's said
The white one halted there, and bowed its head.

There is a sword upon the black one's back,
A crucifix upon the brown one's back,
A golden rug upon the white one's back.

Save for the golden rug its back is bare.
Soon in our time Messiah will ride there.

Translated by Dom Moraes

Stars of the Skies

Stars of the skies so distant, stars of the skies so near,
Lights so distant, distant, from the eye that gazes at them,
Lights so near, so near, to the heart upon them gazing!
Where is it I have seen you and where have I not seen you
On my way through this broad earth, through all the earth's great
    fulness,
On my humble, humble path from my tranquil village birthplace,
That home of good kind people, the fields whence first I wandered—
A youth who wove within him unspoken dreams not granted,
His heart a treasure trove of secret hidden forces,
A wealth of brimming forces at the summit of their splendour—
Until I reached this place, until I stopped—not tired,
Nor weary of my travail, midway along my journey.

Stars of the northern skies, such chill sharp winks exchanging,
Like sparks in the eyes of wolves on long, long nights of autumn,
Above Kyrelia's forests, in the land of wistful beauty,
That called to me and warned me with a glance both near and distant
Among the gloomy pines in the blast of northern tempests
Standing dense and clustered and staring into mirrors
Of holy lakes that age in frames of dampened rockbanks,
Standing dense and crowded, gripped by primal trembling
Since the day that earth and heaven wrought spells so strong and evil
In words forming and performing of ancient incantation
In mighty forces fettered in words that were still young then
When first were framed world's wonders and their mysterious
    secrets.

Stars of Ukrainian steppeland, so beautiful and mournful;
Stars of the green expanse, why so sad and mournful?
Is it from seeing your furrows changing shape so often?
Now a sea, an ocean, of frolicking weeds and grasses,
Scented green and flowing, abounding with life's own wildness;
Now a tossing ocean of corn in changing colours:
Silver, green and orange, all in the threefold blessing
Of rains and of the plough and of the scythe of iron;
Now a boundless span, placeless with no border,
Soil of mighty battles, of human fields of slaughter—
Here the blood of one people dries, and another's blood starts flowing,
And before one field is quenched, the next's already thirsting.

Stars of Crimea accept my blessing! A tent of blackened velvet
Has wrought your lovely framework. The sea, the rock, the forest
All yearn in longing for you, for your secret speech of radiance.
And when the sleeping sea takes your picture to its lap,
Or lifts its peaks of waves and breakers to the skies,
Is it not of you it dreams? Is it not for you my heart longed,
The heart of a youth still green, at the height of early blossom,
Full of stars of his own, full of the song of his future?
Some fell dead and lightless, and some have already darkened
In the evil mist that spreads across the breadths of life.
And some, yes, some still twinkle, far distant, and illumine
With a light of dreams gone by, with the charm of healthful youth.

Stars of Mediterranean night! Stars—Gods of days of old!
Nothing in the world can equal your beauty, your holy radiance.
If the stars of the world are sculpted of precious stones of agate,
Then you are tiny suns, panes in the sky's deep sapphire.
You are the firstborn gods among gods of sea and land.
It was you in man implanted the spirit of knowledge and courage:

The wise of Babylon and the Chaldees heard the singing of your circuits
And divined their combinations, the first of nature's secrets;
It was you inspired courage in those of Sidon and Canaan
To find a way across the sea, into the world's dark mysteries,
To leave their Garden of Eden, to extend and expand its boundaries.
Though man appeared to create—it was they who made him 'Man'.

Stars of the Land of Israel! The day earth and heaven were made,
It is said He appeared in holiness, dressed in ephod and in breastplate.
And you were fixed on that breastplate—you and only you!
Stars of the Land of Israel, stars of Grandfather Israel!
All his days are engraved on you, for you looked down upon him.
The fathers of the people raised their eyes to you for witness.
You alone, from your orbits, in ancient days fought for him,
You beheld his battle, you beheld his greatness,
You behold his misery. In you are joined together
Past and present and future. Oh, you who see so far,
Perhaps even now you behold his future, speak:
What is then the vision and when its end, oh speak!

Stars of shining light past spheres of southern tropics!
Here the 'Southern Cross', and here the great Cantabros.
The first appears in glory—here began the wondrous legends,
The most beautiful of legends that the new man started weaving.
Waters of the ancient ocean—a tray of molten lead,
And transparent fineness of skies. One alone and lonely below,
And its brother lonely above. Without them there is nothing.
Schools and schools of waves, mighty currents rising,
Languid, heavy, murky, and again the ocean gleams
Just as on that first great day, when the world's Creator made
The heavens and the waters of the face of earth's massed hugeness,
And the stars looked down in wonder at the chaos on the earth.

Stars of the ranging pampas, figures strange and alien!
Stars of new lands and skies, that I have never known,
Lights of dread expanses, last witnesses of nature's forces
Forging the mighty beings that you saw wandering here,
Those marvels of first existence, glorious and dreadful monsters,
The wondrous crown of strength of creation not yet perfected.
You beheld the dying of those giants of enormity.
You I do not like, but my heart is drawn towards you,
Towards the wonder of your riddle and the mystery of your being.
And from somewhere a silent sorrow strokes the shrinking heart
That starts to steal away with your entering the heavens:
As though you were only candles of memorial for worlds long dead.

Stars of beloved skies, stars that my mother loved!
Did I receive their names from my father's youthful wanderings
Through nights of summer and autumn along the broadtracked roads
Between the Dnieper and Don, between Black and Caspian Seas?
He knew their many names, all heard from greyhaired travellers;
Showed me 'Alpha' and 'Omega', 'The Great Bear' and 'The Hunter'.
'The Hundred Points of Fire', and 'The Way to the Holy City',—
Simple names and strange that lived their lives in memories
Of simple minded people and the generation's elders
Among names of primitive stars. From my father and my mother
I got my love for you, stars so near and distant.
And I send my blessing to you wherever you are, my friends!

Translated by Richard Flantz

The Last Khuzar

A BALLAD

When spring showers fall to give drink to the plains
That lie soft and swollen and soaking with rains,
Then the river-bed deepens, fills up, overflows,
It foams and is gone—a ravine only shows
The source of its gush, the scene of its spree
As it rips up the fields on its way to the sea.

Beside the ravine a wolf-cub is hurrying
After a hungry she-wolf, pursuing,
Through tangles of saltbush and patches of clover,
On carpets of devilgrass and oats bending over.

Beside the ravine a she-wolf is running
After a fleeting horse, she hungrily hurrying,
Through tangles of saltbush and patches of clover,
On carpets of devilgrass and oats bending over.

Beside the ravine a great stallion gallops;
The rider sits huddled, his feet press the stirrups,
Through tangles of saltbush and patches of clover,
On carpets of devilgrass and oats bending over.

This horseman, alone escaped from the battle
Where to Svyatoslav's troops Khuzars fell like cattle,
The city's in smoke, there is no sanctuary:—
The Khuzar fled for his life, the last one still free,
The last of the converts, the last of the last,
His valiant horse tiring, though galloping fast

Through tangles of saltbush and patches of clover,
On carpets of devilgrass and oats bending over.

His path now is crossed by a bird winging by:
"Heron, O heron, whither do you fly?"
—"To the home of the vulture whose throat is so bald,
To the battle of death, to my last battle I'm called."

Can it be that the king hears the words of the bird?
He lashes his horse, his eyes are all blurred,
His path now is crossed by a galloping deer:
"Reindeer, O reindeer, whither rush you from here?"
—"To the cave of ruins, to the wolf's underground lair,
To the battle of death—I may not return from there!"

Can it be that the king hears the words of the deer?
He pulls on the reins, slow his steed's wild career.
His path now is crossed by a passing grey crow:
"Grey crow, O grey crow! Where do you rush? Whither go?"
—"To the cliff, to grey years, to the nest of passing breath,
With great sorrow I rush to the battle of death!"

Can it be that the king hears the words of the crow?
He turns his horse round, and returns towards the foe.

Translated by Richard Flantz

The Ballad of the Hive

In the heat of the sun's sweet steaming noon hours
All the drones of the hive rock asleep on the flowers.

They dream and they drowse: hearts so broad, hearts so bold,
All around is a humming, a singing echo of gold:

"In the Kingdom of Honey, in the City of Cream,
Lies a Queen fast asleep in a passionate dream.

"The Queen, in all her youth's beauteous bloom,
Lies alone and awaits the approach of her groom;

"For the one of ten thousand the lovely Queen waits;
Her soft fur is made of gold satin and lace.

"She has eyes that are lights, her figure is slender,
The crown on her head is of down of fine splendour.

In the whole of the hive there is no-one so fair,
The blue hive is full of bewitched, scented air,

"It is lined with shadows the hue of deep amber,
Where the rays of the sun, as if erring, meander.

"Only once will she leave her palace's walls,
Only once will she fly in glory that enthralls.

"Only once will she love with all of her soul,
Only once will she give her lover her all,

"Love that is young, love exalted with grace,
But only once to be clasped in a husband's embrace.

"Yes, only once! Yet in her moment then
She'll reward him with all of the love in her ken,

"With her all... Her all for her man, the abyss of her way,
Bound only to him till the last light of her day.

"There is none like her lover, none like her man!
To make her his wife he will give his life's span.

"He will clasp her but once in a converse of bliss:
'I love you,' he'll say, and die in the kiss.

"Nowhere in the world is there love to compare,
Nor one in ten thousand so great and so fair!

"Praise then the lover, that hero so bold,
His honour we'll tell in songs made of gold."

Translated by Richard Flantz

YAAKOV CAHAN

1881—1960

Poet, author and playwright. Born in Slutzk, White Russia, he moved with his family to Poland and pursued his university education in Switzerland, Germany and France (Ph. D.). Returning to Poland, he taught Hebrew at the Jewish high school at Lodz, was inspector of Hebrew secondary schools and lectured in Hebrew literature at the Institute for Jewish Knowledge in Warsaw. He was active in the revival of the Hebrew language and edited literary periodicals, including Hatekufah *and* Sneh. *He settled in Palestine in* 1934 *and was elected chairman of the national chapter of the P. E. N. Club.*

His collected poems, plays, stories and translations have been published in ten volumes. His early poems express joie de vivre, *love of nature, beauty and youth: his lyrical landscape paintings are pervaded by a religious fervour. A later series of poems,* Helvetia, *depicting the Alpine landscape, are charged with a plastic, musical rhythm and an air of legendary myth. His love poems betray the romantic approach of man's yearning for the woman he desires. His national poems,* Hazon haTishbi *('The Vision of Elijah') and* Melech Israel *('King of Israel'), inveigh against pettiness, egoism and Zionist extremism. He lauds the heroism of Jewish rebels in his* Shir HaBiryonim *('Song of the Rebels') poems; he sets out to create a monotheistic myth in* Agadot Elohim *('Divine Legends'); and in* Mahazot Fantastiyim *('Fantastic Visions') he symbolically expresses the universal ideas of man's conflict in the face of purity and defilement, God and Satan.*

*A central motif of Cahan's poetry (*Ariel—A Vision of the Immortality of Man*) is the injustice of death, which casts its shadow over all life. His drama* Beluz *presents the conflict between the world of simplicity and innocence and the mad rush of progress and civilization.* Sefer Elifel, *based on the Atlantis myth, hints at the impending collapse of the modern world.*

He translated into Hebrew Goethe's Torquato Tasso, Faust *and* Iphigenie auf Tauris, *and Heine's* Hebraeische Melodies.

World of Glass

The world is trembling glass, and in the sky
the sun shines, like a glass eye.

The world is ice. No voice, no windy gust.
Even the air subsides. Like glass dust.

No bird, no beast. Fear's freezing nought.
Silence frozen into thought.

Glass trees budding in no spring.
Symbols of themselves, past flowering.

Glass waters heaped in river beds. Glass graves
preserving the dead forms of waves.

The dust of buildings and glass skeletons,
to testify the living lived here once.

As if it were not, the world still stands;
how it exists no one understands.

One pallid shadow only wanders slow,
the shadow of a man who lived long ago.

A rustle of silence, the footsteps of one dead,
advancing with care, halting with every tread,

who glances and passes, moves without aim or will
from field to forest, from forest to hill,

from hill to valley—and ever must pass
glass only, glass only, a desolation of glass.

Without pain or wonder, he must go,
nothing in his face, the nothingness of snow.

No tremor shakes his blood, no dread
makes the hairs stand on his head.

No hint of a smile lights mouth or eye.
The man's shadow—the shadow of him who was I.

Translated by Robert Friend

I Like the Trees Those Nights

I like the trees those nights,
   Those pallid nights
When a moon of magic pours mysterious light
   On mountain and on stream,
   And its waters gleam
Like the face of a giant who has fallen asleep,
   Sheathed in his silver mail.
The whole world is a silver world, asleep
   With its shadows and its lights,
Each nook unfathomable, each shadow with its secrets deep and old,
And every stone held in the spell of silence manifold.

They stand asleep, the trees, and dream;
   Deep is their sleep.
No slightest tremor! From trunk to crown
   Silence is what they are;
   Their life is locked within,
   Their passion is enthralled,
   A passion powerful and free,
   But now enchained.
The light of the moon is peace around them curled;
It freezes upon them, like the cold dream of a silver world.

Translated by Robert Friend

My Heart is not Here...

Fog clouds of anger,
the earth is unclean.
Without consolation,
days, nights without meaning
drag slowly by.
Everywhere whips
of arrogance crack.
My heart is not here
my heart has been silenced.

Translated by Robert Friend

"An Hour will Come..."

An hour will come when the touch of a powerful hand
will fill me with fresh streams, brim me with brightness;
my heart will rise above the vanities of the living;
my soul be purified, suddenly shedding light.

Suddenly the heart will grow strong like a rock and fortress,
from whose fastness sparkling springs break forth;
the whole world will be my home and every creature my brother;
and the tumult of life will be my song of songs.

And in that hour how I shall bless my fortune!
I shall worship my God with an added measure of faith,
accepting gratefully the good vouchsafed me,
accepting even the bad without complaint.

Translated by Robert Friend

YAAKOV FICHMAN

1880—1958

Poet, critic and essayist. He was born in Bessarabia and travelled widely in his youth working at a variety of trades (as a baker's assistant, waiter, porter, carter and village teacher), at the same time writing for various periodicals. For some years he divided his time between Palestine and Europe (Warsaw, Kishinev, Vilna, Odessa and Berlin), before he settled in Palestine in 1925. He edited literary periodicals and anthologies.

An aesthete and impressionist, he has a keen eye for all that is colourful in life. His lyrical verse, pervaded with an air of calm sadness, displays an intense love of life. He is a master of description, evinced in his songs of the sea and pen-portraits of the Israel landscape. His love poems are charged with longing, sadness and reminiscence. He also wrote lyrical verse on biblical and historical subjects, indirectly voicing his feelings on current matters. His literary criticism aesthetically emphasizes the beauty inherent in the works he discusses.

His collected poems appeared under the following titles: Givolim *('Stalks'),* Yemey Shemesh *('Days of Sunshine'),* Tzelalim al Sadot *('Shadows on the Fields'),* Aviv-Be-Shomron *('Spring in Samaria'),* Pinat Sadeh *('Corner of the Field'). He wrote numerous critical and biographical works, including two on the poetry and life of Bialik.*

He compiled a number of chrestomathies, and translated into Hebrew Hebbel's 'Herod and Miriam', poems of Heine, Goethe, Duhamel and Bunin, and prose works of Hermann Hesse and Jens Peter Jacobsen.

Jerusalem

Jerusalem! Cry of the hungry heart, oblivion's
garden beyond the hills when refugees fled the storm—
Silence you are, submission and rebellion.
Because of you, heart shudders, the griefs swarm.

By green of your earth I swear and by your sunlight.
I inherit the desolation that remains.
I stand like a tree in stone, by you held spellbound—
soul woven with soul, my root in your dry veins.

I love what survives in you as in cold lava,
the rejoicing sound of ancient days,
echoing still from your white rocks of silence.

But with your holiness is now my strife,
and I have come to smash rocks into clods.
Dead splendour rests on furrows of new life.

Translated by Robert Friend

The Secrets of the Landscape

It is hardly enough to stir and to mix
with a matching hand the pinks and the blues,
in effervescent colours fix
landscapes on canvas, all sorts of views.
What is scattered, gather; listen and remember;
arrest the moments before they flee;
a landscape captures the secret wonder,
the world's renewal in what you see.
False treasure like trash you must cast on the midden,
and the vain loveliness that led you astray;
rescue the little (that in hints hidden,
in the riddles of your dark blood kept from the day,
holds in its heart the secret, the glory).
One mastering stroke of your brush will lay bare
the world's dear things long lost and long buried.
Delve in that darkness and do not despair:
in that are *you*. The runes declare
the root of loveliness, the best of treasure.

Translated by Robert Friend

Mount Nevo

I have caused thee to see it with thine eyes,
but thou shalt not go over thither.

Deuteronomy 34:4.

The sun descends, the land breathes rest
Before the hush of Nevo's crest,
But a dim voice under the hill
Cries out, and I am restless still.

The night draws near. Time to depart.
It is too late to rage, O heart.
He whom the day gave of its best
Returns at eve to an empty nest.

I shall not beg compassion, pray
For the thin grace of one more day.
Hidden in rock and silence, I
With my redeemèd here shall lie.

Here I shall fall with them. How all
The shore grows white when night must fall!
How calm in me my fires have grown,
Gentle the world with oblivion!

Whose wide heart yearned for a wide land must
Bequeath to a narrow plot his dust.
Release is what his suffering craves?
The bed is good in Nevo's caves.

Translated by Robert Friend

Eve

I love Adam. He is brave of heart,
his blood is generous; and he, like God,
is wise. But the serpent whispers things
that are so strange. They hurt—and they caress.

When Adam sleeps, Eden lies desolate;
its birds are silent and its grass is wet.
And then *he* kindles, calling from the thicket,
a bonfire in my heart. "Pick it! Pick it!"

How good to feel at dawn Adam's warm hand
caress my flesh again, and in the hush
listen to the coursing of its blood,
But every bush of day that drinks the light
bends to a darkness. Eden is enchanted
only till night awakes the shadow in the brush.

Translated by Robert Friend

The Sail

Who am I? A white, lonely sail;
on black waters I wander and sing through my shrouds.
The black waters greet me; the night winds are friends;
and friends are the clouds.

Where? Green waves of the abyss
murmur of splendid lands and distant bays;
captive of the winds, I wander many days—
every isle, every shore promising bliss.

I am a white sail on the empty reaches,
hailing the headlands of night, the desolate beaches.
With a song for each day, a hold full of ease—
I roam with the homeless winds of the seas.

Translated by Robert Friend

The River

Sometimes to a late September river,
lonely with murmuring thoughts that have no end,
upon an evening that is hushed and golden,
flocks of anonymous birds descend.

Soft, radiant of hue (with all the favour
the hungry heart has yearned for since the spring),
one after one, they light upon the river,
charmed by its evening, its riddles still untold.

So unexpectedly, so surprisingly,
—in joy? in sorrow?—see, they cling.
It is to you that all the birds have come.

Though sunk completely in its silent bed,
the river welcomes them, and to the profound
depth listens, its darkness golden-crowned.

Translated by Robert Friend

When from the Ark...

When from the ark, redeemed and blessed,
Noah went forth with beast and beast
bounding about him in their strength and joy
(survivors of a world forever drowned
who weave the coming days, from whom the future flowers)
he lifted silently his questioning eyes
to invisible distances. What had the deep,
retreating, left behind for blossoming?

His heart leaped at the sight
of this new earth, fresh as the spring,
from which the waters multitudinous
had washed the filth of ages; a virgin land
smiling with the sweetness
of valley brightness and of forest darkness,
of pathless mountains of delight
no wandering foot had trod,
no eye had gazed upon,
a meadowland of grass without a yesterday,
without a history,
where fear had not yet cast
shadow or cloud.

His heart took courage then,
and he sent forth
into the landscape opening up before them,
his dear companions, to explore
that blossoming world and drink again

from its goblets newly filled. He hears
the murmuring doves above his head,
the roar of lions leaping towards the distance.
Even the sound of water, mother of so much evil,
comes like the sound of music to his ears.

But when the beating of his heart subsided,
he heard the painful cry
of a world lost in the silence.
Bleating of sheep wild waters swirled away
(innocence shining in the dying eye),
the weeping of a child torn from the breast
and sucked with his mother into the deep—
these echoed in his ear in the brilliance of the day.
How was the world to be renewed
when a bereaved mother and her child
had sunk in waters with their blood imbrued?

But the world that once had drowned
went on to bloom again,
and on the wrath of every naked rock,
the earth brought forth the grass of joy.
Rivers turned golden,filled with happiness
the heart of a world that would not stop for thought.
And from the endless spaces
winds brought tenderness
unknown so many springs.
He listened then
to his blood's imploring voices:
Sun, blot out the deep and its deep shadows!
Earth, gather into yourself the scattered blood!
How can an eye that saw a whole world drown
behold once more the flood?

The man arose and lifted up his eyes.

On every side he saw a land in leaf,
its every furrow green and fruitful every tree—
with only one bald slope,
a single blotch upon the blossoming landscape,
a scar of sorrow on the blessed earth.
Then shaking off his grief,
the man arose and with his hoe in hand,
blood singing in him, spoke:
'This is an omen for my heart to read,
a covenant of its redemption.
Here will I plant a vineyard, a green tent,
Shade in this place will water burning sand,
shade clothe the nakedness of rock and cliff,
shade cover every horror of the deep:
shade that conceals the shadows of a world that died!—
then will the grief of the world be swallowed up,
then will joy blossom for me like a bride.'

Thus did the man toil
among the mounds of earth
to dig his shadow a grave and cover it.
Thus did he bury it,
deep in the lap of mountain soil.

Translated by Robert Friend

Abishag

I waste my teeming age. I do not know
when crops grow golden and the earth brings forth.

Early the world arises there to blossom,
but here my days fall silently like leaves.

My woods of chastity grow taller daily,
rustling sadly—without a bird of song.

In castle splendour, in imperial purple,
a locust wilderness devours my bloom.

I leave my chamber, and like lips that burn
the dazzle of the white day welcomes me.

The heat of gardens, fronds dancing in the sun,
ignite a fire rising in my blood.

Peering from the secrecy of casements,
the unseen eyes of princes kiss my footsteps.

And then sometimes a tenderness floats in me,
my heavy blossom aches,

And all my unconceiving, unattempted flesh
—a vine neglected—yearns the gatherer.

But when night finds me sleepless and my eye
pierces the darkness of the frozen castle,

like a bird in its morning nest, a world then stirs,
the king's heart plays upon the fiddle strings.

This splendour hiding in wrinkles of pale day
rises from ashes when night's glory sings.

Night's castle sinks, and grief is drowned in grief
as wave is drowned in wave. And every sound

calling my poverty from the midnight dark
is gathered with it to the caves of song.

O song of midnight! in which my blood flows purely
(as sap in tender branches) to the dawn.

All of my warmth I give to the old King—
his heart plays the weeping of my Spring.

Translated by Robert Friend

AVRAHAM BEN-YITZHAK

1883—1950

Poet. Born in Przemysl, Galicia, studied at the Universities of Berlin and Vienna and obtained his Ph. D. In 1914 he became lecturer in Hebrew and Psychology at the Jerusalem Teachers' Training College and later went to Vienna, where he stayed till the end of the First World War. After the war he worked for the Zionist Executive in London and was for some time political adviser to the late Chaim Weizmann, later returning to Vienna where he became principal of the Teachers' College. He settled in Palestine in 1938.

His few poems were collected after his death from various publications and published in book form in 1952. They are the early harbingers of modernism in Hebrew poetry, in the spirit of Hofmannsthal, Rilke and Valery. The main elements in his poetry consist of a symbolistic aestheticism, delicate imagery, musical tone, expressiveness and the free use of blank verse.

Kingdom

The daylight flickers on my crown,
Whose gold burdens my forehead,
The edges of my robe wash over the marble staircase,
The sea moans its fine evening grief.

Night's daughter, come quietly,
Sit at my feet on marble whiteness.
Let the wind lift your hair,
Such black hair.
The waters are rising:
Stay quiet
Till I tell you: Get up and sing.

Translated by Arthur Jacobs

The Lonely Say

One day leaves a flickering sun for the next,
Night mourns night.
Summer after summer is gathered in falling leaves
While the world sings its pain.

To-morrow we shall die and have no more speaking:
As the day we set out, face a gate, closing.
When the heart exults it is God who draws us,
But fearing sacrilege—repents.

One day lifts a burning sun for the next,
Nights pour out their stars.
A few lonely lips hold their song.
On seven paths we are divided, come home by one.

Translated by A. C. Jacobs

Bright Winter

The world is clean, hard and white.
The wind from the north yesterday scattered
The purposeless,
Blind and wandering
Dreams of mist.
Today the wind holds back its breath.
All round snow glints,
Deep blue shadows are on the mountains,
The pale blue skies
In their light, quiver.
In shadow,
The river extends
Trapped in its frozen beauty,
Ice of dimmed emerald
And bright glowing snows,
Till its curved green
Track is lost, there
In distance.
Daylight takes fire there
And its pieces of flame glitter
As though a sun had fallen
On mass ice figures,
Hardened like crystal,
And been broken.
I closed my eyes.
My blood in me
Makes music, rings

In my ears:
The world is clean.

It feels
As though my own heart
Beats with the earth's heart,
And travels the streams
That flow under the pelt of ice.

A clean world,
Clean.

Translated by A. C. Jacobs

Blessed Are Those Who Sow And Do Not Reap

Blessed are those who sow and do not reap
Because they wander far.

Blessed are those who give themselves freely, the splendour
Of whose youth has added to daylight
Though they flung off their glory where roads part.

Blessed are those whose pride crosses the borders of their souls
And becomes a white humility
After the rainbow's rising in the cloud.

Blessed are those who know what their heart cries out in deserts
And on whose lips silence flowers.

Blessed are they, for they will be taken into the heart of the world
Wrapped in a cloak of unremembrance,
Forever remaining without speech.

Translated by A. C. Jacobs

The Mountains Grouped Around My Town

The mountains standing grouped around my town
Have a secret hidden in their forests:
There is the sea of trees' rushing above
And in shadow, below, the hidden secret.

Came vintage
With gold force
And scattered light around.
All the narrow tracks lightened.
The forest took on brightness.
It was tall and quiet,
Head in the sky.
Over its secret
Slept light.

Translated by A. C. Jacobs

I Didn't Know My Soul

In this vintage season, when the skies are full of movement,
Rays of light are thrown out by the earth,
Grey, wasting clouds are driven
Wide winged by the storm.
From the greenish black of the forest
Your house emerges doubly pale in its isolation,
Calling me with its windows:
In my heart
Is shelter from the storm.

When you are sitting by the earth,
And its gold dances
On the deep brown of your bent head
Light flows between your fingers,
And the flame reflects movement
In the black silk of your dress.
Silently apples lie burning on your table,
Yellow grapes cluster thickly in their basket,
There is the full scent of blessing.

Let the forest thunder and roar,
Its song is sweet
In the stillness
Of your loved corner.

You and I,
With the sea's din
Over us,

Concealed
Like two pearls
In their soil
On the bed of the sea.

I didn't know my soul.
It took its fill of silence.
Look, my spirit's wings flutter.
The forest may roar and thunder,
The wind strike its waves,
While your quivering look rests on me.
In you is blessing
And comfort,
Though the storm cried at my soul,
Listen, there is a howling of breakers in the forest,
The whole earth is cried on;
The world has set all its soul bare
Before God in the storm.

Translated by A. C. Jacobs

YEHUDA KARNI

1884—1949

Poet and journalist. Born in Pinsk, Poland, he was active in the Zionist movement from an early age, and wrote poems in Hebrew, Yiddish and Russian. In 1921 he settled in Palestine and served on the editorial staff of Ha'aretz, where he wrote a regular column on current affairs and for twenty-five years published feuilletons and poems satirizing unfavourable aspects in the life of the country. His works include:

She'arim ('Gateways')—a collection of poems written abroad, on love and nature, national pathos charged with prayer and reproach of God and man, and tending towards mysticism.

Besha'arayich, Moledet ('In thy Gates, O Homeland')—a collection of poems imbued with the poet's love for his poor, desert land.

Yerushalayim—a series of poems expressing ardent love for the eternal, craggy city of Jerusalem.

Shir VaDema *('Song and Tears')—lamentation for the European holocaust.*

Evening

The evening here does not steal in in secret
With the cat;
The cloak of night's no swaddling gift of soft velvet,
No welcome mat.

The evening here does not maul hearts, to maul and suck
Drop after drop down to the final spark;
Night's curtain does not fall down stuck
Between the marked and that which does not bear the mark.

The evening here informs, then binds and slays and hurries
To night's dark nave;
The night then grinds and flays and buries
And seals the grave.

Translated by Richard Flantz

Wedge Me into the Fissure

Wedge me into the fissure with each fallen stone.
Hammer me till I grow strong.
Perhaps I shall appease my land and atone
For the people's sin: the ruins unmended so long.

To be one of the stones of my city is all my desire.
Were my bones knitted in with the wall, how glad I would be.
Is my body less than my soul, that through water and fire
Stayed by the people, who shrieked or went silently?

With the stones of Jerusalem wedge me into the wall.
Clothe me in mortar, and from
The very depths of the stones my bones shall call
Till the Messiah come.

Translated by Dom Moraes

Each Stone

Each stone in you gashes,
Stabs
And goads;
And the cold that breaks out
Of your buildings,
Your heights scratched bare,
Rubble, or shafted tombs
Of shut-in caves,
Strikes me as searing flame.
I lie flat on rock, weakened in spirit,
And rise with lips cracked, my forehead marked,
As though I had clutched death's rock
And embraced hell
Among eternity's hills.
Each stone stabs like the Gehenna
In you, Jerusalem,
Yet why, when I rise from that inferno's hold
Do the heavens stand opened to me?

Translated by A. C. Jacobs

Feast

We sat together at one festive board,
and ate bran bread.

The wine-maker sat with us, his jaws full.
But we drank only water from the well.

By weight the bread we ate was portioned out.
Pure was the water from the well mouth.

Nevertheless we were not sad at heart,
and every sip was sweet,

because we knew: one hidden and important
was sitting with us, attentive and observing,

and he, the invisible, dealt out the portions,
not to be changed.

We knew this too: that with our deprivation
he willed us vision.

Translated by Robert Friend

After the Close

I affirm reality after the close,
And though I know that all that grows
Is doomed to dissolution,
I live in the illusion,
That what is not lost will not be lost.

From the beginning I know the last:
That in everything living—death is reflected,
But by this knowledge am not deflected:
I see the bitter end, not at all aghast;
And when death whispers to me and jeers,
I whisper love in women's ears.

Translated by Richard Flantz

Midnight

Midnight. In the house somewhere an old
Woman coughs, and I hear a child wail.
It's as though a door suddenly creaked
And someone burst out from a prison cell.

I will go and comfort the racked woman
And quiet down the screaming of the child.
I'll tell them that my soul has left off feeling:
For the three of us a jackal's howling wild.

The woman in the darkness lies there moaning
The child cries, and the jackal howls his plight.
World, stupid world, and understanding,
To cry for nothing halfway through the night.

Translated by A. C. Jacobs

Honey

Yellow, sticky, sweet is honey:
Yellow,
Sticky,
Sweet;
And the heart beating here is still mellow,
Frisky,
Deep,
Still so pure, so fresh, so sunny.

To what can I compare the quality of honey?—
Amity,
Love,
Affection;
And the son of Adam and the daughter of Eve,
Like the untiring bees that buzz above,
Scrape the hives out to perfection,
To make clear crystals of their honey.

Translated by Richard Flantz

DAVID SHIMONI

1886—1956

Poet. Born in White Russia, he came to Palestine in 1909 and worked as a labourer and watchman. After studying philosophy and semitic languages at German universities, he settled in Palestine in 1921 and taught at a secondary school.

A sober poet, his verse is frequently a commentary on current events. His early verse was lyrical, filled with Zionist yearning, expressing his distress at the rootlessness of Jewish youth in the Diaspora and indicating the latent forces seeking an outlet. His songs of travel (a series of lyrically descriptive poems) express a craving for the great wide world, its wealth and splendour, and contain beautiful descriptions of seascapes and desert reaches. Eshet Iyov ('Job's Wife'), a poem with a distinctly moral basis, is the accusation of a woman who will not reconcile herself with God so long as there is pointless suffering in the world. Sefer ha-Idylliot ('The Book of Idylls'), written in Palestine, is brighter, dealing chiefly with the idyllic character of the Palestinian landscape and the life of the pioneers of the various Aliyot, against a background of swamp and desert, memories of the past and present-day ideologies.

Shimoni also wrote parables and satires—Bisheviley Habivar ('Along the Paths of the Menagerie'), where he castigates current social, political and artistic events. Be-Hashai ('In Secret') is a collection of poetic meditations. Moledet ('Homeland') is a series of stories about the Palestinian scene. Ahavat Shlomo ('Solomon's Love'), Armilos Harasha ('The Evil Armalos'), Sefer Hapoemot ('Book of Poems'), Pirhei Zichronot ('Reminiscences'), Hevlo Shel Meshiah ('Messianic Pangs'), and Me'al Haduchan ('From the Pulpit'). His collected poems have appeared in a number of editions.

He translated Lermontov's selected poems into Hebrew.

And Should the Wonder Happen

And should the wonder happen and I live on
To see the world illumined with new light,
The light of justice, love and peace,
I shall surely praise that generation
From the depths of my sorrow, from the deepest abyss
Of my shattered soul,
But my wound will not be healed.
Its blood will flow as long as my heart beats,
As the blood of my brothers flowed, till their hearts froze...

And should I be granted the right to hear
The Redeemer's trumpet blast, and to see my people
Flowering in their redeemed land,
All free and fresh and radiant with a light supreme,
And a vast world rising from their glow—
I shall surely rejoice to have been a doorstep
To this generation of redemption. But still from my song of freedom
A stifled moan will burst,
Will tremble and resound, as long as my heart beats,
As the moans of my brothers trembled
Until their souls departed...

And even should the miracle of miracles occur,
And the dead rise from their graves,
And all my martyred people live:
The splattered, the strangled and the charred,
And all my tortured, ravaged sisters—
And should they float in lustrous glory,

Radiant with the dew of immortality,
Flooding out all darkness with their splendid laughter—
Yet my heart, as long as my heart beats,
Shall walk in darkness, that same darkness
That enwrapped my brothers as they were led to slaughter.

And even should God in all His mercy
Offer me the cup of forgetfulness—
I will not touch it! I shall say: "Forgive me, God!
But if I taste of the cup of forgetfulness,
I will be no longer I!...
And so, as long as my heart beats,
And as long as I know not why
You have done all that You have done—
I am unable to forget, I am unwilling to forget!..."

Translated by Richard Flantz

Into a Blazing Desert

Into a blazing desert, flung from a sling, despairing,
My lips all parched with thirst, my soul forgetting joys,
Just night and day my nails upon the rockface scratching:
Arise, arise, my spring! O spring, O spring, arise!

And in the depths of the rock my soul could already hear
The sound of the secret source, the tinkling flow of crystal,
And I but a pace away from the wonder, now so very near.
But my heart was getting weaker, my strength was growing dull.

With the remnant of my soul's sorrow, from my body's decrepitude,
To the spring in the rock's dark bowels, I poured my pleading wail:
'Grant me but one droplet of your abundant plenitude,
And with redoubled vigour I'll redeem you from your goal!'

Then from the depths a sad voice lamented, whispering:
'Alas, I cannot give my plenty in vessel or in measure.
If you can only reach me, all yours shall be my spring,
But while the rock is between us, I can give none of my treasure.'

And the sun above my head blazes down with open jowls,
I scratch the face of the rock, and my soul in its pain-filled flood
Knows that if I reach the spring, the spring in the rock's dark bowels,
Its first drop will turn red with the last drop of my blood.

Translated by Richard Flantz

Whenever I See Children

Whenever I see children in merry shouting throngs,
Their eyes so gay and radiant with the fresh joy of pure hearts,
And I hear their lilting laughter, this world's bright song of songs,
That from their innocent souls so uninhibited starts—

Then with the breath of spring, distant, wondrous, sacred,
With the scent of the sweetest dew of an early vibrant morning,
The gloom of autumn sadness sucks my soul in secret,
And the bitter fear of night sets my heart to trembling.

But not for this, as my sun sets, is my soul sad,
Not that no more will the east glow red for me,
Not that no more can I be like them, those children glad,
Not that my days are forfeit to a tyrannous destiny—

But for this I grieve—that you will be like me, my dears,
That your springs will turn murky, just like my clouded stream,
That your pure dew, ah yes, will also turn to tears,
That a cold and hostile world will freeze your laughter and your
   dreams.

And in the essence of pain my soul prays silently and long:
If it is not for the sake of weeping that we perch over the abyss—
Then for the sake of a baby's laugh, the world's bright song of songs,
Over your world, Lord God, pour a little warmth and bliss...

Translated by Richard Flantz

] 142 [

If Only

A young swallow strayed into a noisy town,
And from his rooftop nest looked down
And heard the city's many sounds,
And felt so proud when he found
That as his ear took in the city's din
Its hearing sharpened, and he could sing
Out loud, and so clearly could these sounds repeat,
That with every winged songster he'd compete.
Then after months of wandering he returned
To the fields of his homeland, where he learned
That the nightingale, to his surprise,
Was still the most loved warbler of the skies.
"You're all just peasants, unprogressive,
Sunken in ignorance as in mud,
And you don't know and you don't see
That the nightingale's song is dying out
In all the cities of the sea,
In every place that's been reached at all
By what is truly cultural.
Hurrah! Capitals, metropoles
Beyond the seas!
There alone is the surging source
Of life in all its force!
The sound of engines, the blast of planes,
The shattering, battering, chattering roar!
After all these is there a point any more
To the irrelevant chant of nightingales?
And by the way, in the new song,
That I have brought you from my travels long,

You'll surely notice with clarity
The pulse of cities, fierce and free;
I'm willing to sing it now, as you see,
(It's the epitome of poesy!)
But on one condition I'll insist:
That the nightingale from song desist,
And remain silent as from now..."
But the nightingale laughed from on his bough:
"—Why, O Swallow, do you rage at me?
I'm sure the city's melody
Is varied, lovely, heavenly,
I'm sure your voice, so loud and strong,
Was born just for the city's song,
I'm sure that I, a humble peasant,
Am unworthy to sing the urban chant,
But why should it bother you if in my own woods
I softly sing my melodic moods?
And if I'm not troubled, before you begin,
That your mighty voice, strong from storm and din,
Will put my faint warbling in the shade,
Why then, why should you be afraid
That your marvellous melody
Will be swallowed up because of me?...
For after all, in the sky's spacious bounds
There's room enough for the song of towns
And for the chant of furrowed ground.
So, noble citizen, let your voice ring,
Sing out your song of power and lightning!
If only———
If only, apart from shattering, battering, chattering—
You also knew how to sing..."

Translated by Richard Flantz

From the Tales of a Sick Youth

[I] HE DIDN'T KEEP HIS WORD

How is it possible my father could mislead me?
That good man, so dear, so lovable,
whose only teachings were truth and honesty,
who never profaned his mouth with a single lie?
Hating deceit more than he hated death,
how is it possible he could deceive me?

True, all the time my father had implored me
to jump from the train in which we were herded like cattle.
"Jump," he cried, "God may have mercy on you..."
Had his throat grown harsh with thirst
that his voice sounded broken, like a death-rattle?
My heart leaped in my side as if it were cursed.

"I am old and worn-out. No longer strong.
I cannot go with you." And his voice quavered.
"But you, my son, are young.
Maybe the merit of your fathers will save you.
I can only do you more harm than good.
Jump. Run. Hide in the wood."

How the train flew! On either side
the forest extended, a rushing darkness.
Stench, suffocation, horror inside.
And everywhere the spasms of the dying.
My father looked at me: his grief was endless.
I held him, crying, "I shall never leave you!"

] 145 [

A silence. Then a strong voice that surprised me.
"The train is slowing down. It will be climbing.
Quick. Jump. Now is the time.
Quick. I am right behind you." Perfect timing.
Trembling, he pushed me, giving me no choice.
"Quick. Into the bushes. I am right behind you."

That sudden strength of his? Where had it come from?
My heart first froze, then melted in its pain.
Where was my father? How could my father do it?
He had not kept his word.
The train now picked up speed. Before I knew it,
the train was gone and not a sign remained.

And of my father not a sign remained...
Perhaps some ashes somewhere in the fields...
Only his touch, the strong push of his hand
making me leap—deceiving me!—
that scalds my back still with a terrible flame;
that sears my back, and my heart, to this very day.

But amazement more than the fire of that touch burns me:
"He was my father—and he deceived me?"
How am I therefore to be considered mad
that I wish to summon my father to a judgment;
that night and day I cry:
How could my honest father so mislead me?

Translated by Robert Friend

"Why are you always walking, walking and always trembling?"
Thus do they question me, and question me in wonder.
By all that's holy, tell me: Are your thoughts then so unclouded?
Do you not feel that the earth, the earth entirely,
endlessly shivers and shakes, endlessly trembles?
It is not I who moves. It is the whole earth moving.

Why do you look at me thus? Are my words such a puzzle?
Or perhaps you do not know the reason for the trembling?
Has this thought crossed your mind: the Messiah has blown his horn,
and all the dusty dead are breaking out of their graves,
breaking out of their graves and making their way towards Israel?
If so, you are mistaken: the Messiah has not come.

If so, then you must listen... I shall reveal the secret
of why the earth is trembling and never will stop trembling.
No, no, it is not the dead that make the whole world shake.
Rather the countless number of all the living Jews.
Perhaps you have been spared, and have not shared that vision,
but I have not been spared, have seen with my own eyes.

I have seen Jews so many that they could not be numbered,
digging, beaten with sticks, digging and digging pits,
pits enormous and deep.
And when they had finished digging—kicked by boots, they were
    ordered
to stand by those self-same pits.
And as they stood at the edge there, a volley of shots rang out.

Into the pits they had dug the numberless diggers tumbled.
Once more, a group of Jews, beaten with sticks stood there,
and buried their brothers. Slap, slap and smack of spades,
and cries from out the pit. Not all of them had died.
Some had been wounded only, some not even scratched,
but the pits kept filling with earth, the earth kept endlessly moving.

Since then, wherever I go, the earth beneath my foot-soles
is always shaking and trembling.
How shall I not leap with it, when it is always leaping?
Why do you whisper then: the boy is mad?
Is it that you can't feel how they, how they are moving?
Therefore it is not I, but you who have turned mad!

Translated by Robert Friend

If you won't believe me, don't,
but today I spoke with Him. I spoke—
with God.

At last I spoke.

For after all, I had called out
to Him, and called incessantly.
Called day and night.
Shouted, whispered, wept.
Had begged for mercy and had raised my voice—
and pleaded.
How I had pleaded and pleaded,
and He seemed not to hear.

And it was then—when the fields had begun to move,
and my father and I were already back in the ghetto,
for the murderers had failed to murder us—
when under the fields with thousands of other Jews,
my mother and my little brother, and my two sisters too,
were moving—
it was then—when the fields had begun to move—
that I cried out to Him, cried out to my God.

I do not know
if anyone heard my cries
in that night in the dark ghetto—
perhaps because thousands were crying and wailing,
or because the silence was so great,
and my cry too was silent.

I do not know
if anyone heard my cry;
but He heard, God heard,
and never answered me.

And on the next day, when they were taking us
in their cars of death,
and my dear father, that holy man, persuaded me to jump
into the wood,
persuaded me and betrayed me
(for in spite of his promise he did not go with me)—
on the next day in the wood,
at night in the wood,
how I cried out to Him, how I cried out to Him,
to God.

It was night, it was dark in the wood.
And bitter cold.
And there was thirst and hunger.
Many stars.
I did not feel the cold
I was not hungry, was not thirsty.
And did not fear the coming of wild beasts,
not even Germans.
I only looked up at the stars
with longing.
Longing for my father and my mother,
my brother and my sisters.
I looked up at the stars
and cried out to God.

But the stars whispered to me:
Do not cry out to God.
Whisper like us.
God likes it when we whisper to Him...
and I spoke in whispers.
I whispered to Him of the moving fields,
and of the cars of death,
the furnaces,
of everything, of everything.

And asked Him why my father had deceived me,
my dear father, that holy man,
and wept
until the stars wept too—
perhaps they were not stars
but souls—
until the earth that I was lying on
grew wet with tears.
He did not answer me.

How do I know how I was brought here
to this house?
I do not know.
But here I stopped my crying out to God.
Here they think of me as mad.
Perhaps He also thinks of me as mad?
And I stopped crying out to Him.

But this morning, lying half-asleep it seems,
I was shaken broad-awake.
A hand stroking my forehead wakened me.
I opened eyes and saw

a tall old man was bending over me,
his white beard on my face
as white and soft as wool,
his hand in mine.
Knew him at once:
"God!
At last You have answered me. You have come to me at last!'

And I wept.
From the day of my coming here
I had not shed one tear,
And now I wept like a stream.
I wept and I asked
about the moving fields,
the furnaces—
about everything, everything.
And asked Him why my father had deceived me,
my dear father, that holy man...
And asked Him why
HE   HE   HE
had done all that.
I spoke in a whisper,
for so the stars had taught me
to speak to Him.
I may have cried out suddenly,
for He, stroking my head and forehead,
said to me:
"Dear child, I am the doctor only, the doctor only..."

Ha, ha. He the doctor only.
I am not fooled...
And suddenly His face grew red,

and from His eyes the tears began to fall
upon my face.
He wept so much, He wept so much
until I pitied Him,
until my heart grew heavy with my pity,
and I stopped questioning Him.
And then He went away.

But He will come again, will come again,
He said explicitly that He would come.
And when He does, I will not let Him go,
I will not let Him go...
And I shall speak right out and to the point:
God!
Didn't I once feel pity for You?
Why don't You pity us?

Translated by Robert Friend

AVIGDOR HAMEIRI

1887—

Poet, novelist and playwright. Born in Hungary (Carpatho-Russia), he attended the Yeshiva of Pressburg and the Rabbinical College in Budapest. He served as an officer in the Hungarian army in World War I and was taken prisoner by the Russians. In 1921, he settled in Palestine, where he founded and published the one-man literary reviews Lev Hadash *('New Heart') and* Ha-Machar *('The Morrow'). He also founded* Kumkum, *the first Hebrew satirical theatre in the country.*

An expressionist poet, with a keen observation of life, whose work combines the personal with the collective national elements. Alongside the individual element, as expressed in his poems of love and passion, of the joy of life and magical spell of nature, there stands the collective element, sharply brought out in his poetry inveighing against human baseness, egosim and pettiness. Some of his poems strike a reminiscent chord touching upon his experiences in Hungary and as a Russian prisoner of war in Siberia; others with a Palestine setting, are distinctly publicistic in nature and are charged with unbridled enthusiasm and pathos. His verse has been published in numerous collections.

His poems appeared under the titles Halev Em *('Mother's Milk'),* Hamoked Haran *('The Singing Hearth'),* Belivnat Hasapir *('The Whiteness of the Sapphire').*

A prolific writer, he has also written a large number of stories and novels. Two collections of his tales, Ha-Shiggaon ha-Gadol *('The Great Madness'),* Beshem Rabbe Yeshu MiNatzeret *(In the Name of Reb Jesus of Nazareth'),* Hohmat Behemot *('The Wisdom of Cattle'),* Tenuva *'(Yield'),* Hamashiah Halavan *('The White Messiah'),* Ben Laila ve-Laila *('Between Night and Night') and* Gehinnom shel Mattah *('Hell on Earth'), incorporating his first world war reminiscences, depict the fate of a Jewish soldier serving in an army of gentiles, hated both by the enemy and by his own comrades. In* Massa be-Europa ha-Perait *('Journey in*

Barbaric Europe') he records his impressions of pre-World War II Europe. Ha-Mashiah ha-Lavan *('The White Messiah'), a novel set in the European holocaust, warns of the dangers to humanity of the racial theory.* Tenuva *('Yield') is a novel depicting the life of the Palestine pioneers after World War I. In* Sodo shel Socrates *('Socrates' Secret'), set in ancient Greece, the writer propounds the view that Socratic philosophy was influenced by the ancient Hebrew culture.*

He translated into Hebrew works of Schiller, Heine, Max Brod, Arnold Zweig, Stefan Zweig and Haszek.

Rains

Rains—
And in my ears a grieving soul whispers:
What a futile life, passed without doing,
And what an endless tomorrow is coming;
Nothing, rains.
And I, bewildered, in the nets.

Rains—
And a hassidic melody curls in my window.
I shall drown my weary eyes in the heights,
In skies of nothingness, in the nought of nights,
In the rains,
Thanking my God, Almighty God, my Rock and my Maker.

Translated by Richard Flantz

Stillness

The sun is red. It drowses,
Reclining, like me.
Stillness.

Both my eyes fixed on the ridges,
Above me a couple of crows.
Stillness.

In my brain an earthworm,
Sated, sleeps.
Stillness.

The sun is red. It drowses,
Reclining, like me.
Stillness.

Translated by Richard Flantz

Song of the Pioneer

My coat is ragged, worn and fading,
My hair twists in the night wind's raging,
My heart is wounded, torn and bleeding.
Oh my friend,
Tell me, where is all this leading?

My soul is like the troubled foam,
My skull a dull, thick, copper cone,
There are no clothes, there is no home.
Oh my friend,
Tell me, where have God and beauty gone?

There is hope—but it soon is lost,
There is song—but it soon grows hoarse,
And the spirit shivers in the frost—
Oh my friend,
Tell me, what is the word 'homeland' worth?

Translated by Richard Flantz

That Night

Someone knocks upon my window,
And calls with merry singing breath:
Hallo! This is death.

I am startled, but rise, and smile
(Mustn't show fear or dither):
Wait! Let's go together.

The merry voice replies with glee,
Tinkling like bells in clear spring air:
Hurry, or you won't get there.

I stumble, rise, then rush and bustle,
While Vega stares down from heaven:
No no, wait a second.

Silence. An August night, night of my birth,
I march outside, stepping briskly:
Come, let's run, quickly.

So we both run, laughing, upwards,
From below a woman's wailing pours:
He forgot to shut the door.

Translated by Richard Flantz

ZALMAN SHNEOUR

1887—1959

Poet and novelist. Of White Russian birth, he attended heder *and a State secular school, and began publishing poems at an early age. By the time he was* 17 *his first volume of poetry* Im Shekiat He-Hamah *('At Sunset') had appeared. At the age of* 19 *he went to West Europe to study the humanities and sciences at the Sorbonne, was interned by the Germans as a Russian national on the outbreak of World War One, and studied medicine at the University of Berlin. He later settled in Paris, went into hiding during the German invasion of World War Two, and managed to escape to America in* 1941. *In* 1951 *he settled in Israel.*

He wrote in Hebrew and in Yiddish. Some of his novels have been trans-lated into as many as sixteen languages. His collected works in Hebrew have appeared in ten volumes: four volumes of poetry and drama, four volumes of novels and stories, and two of literary criticism and biographies.

His poetry is both intellectual and sensual, expressionistic and filled with pathos, covering a vast range of universal, individual, ethical, meta-physical, as well as specifically Jewish, problems. The erotic element, which he regards as life's prime force, is characteristic of his verse. He is a master of the descriptive art, with his vivid, colourful descriptions of persons and landscapes, of East European Jewish communities and Alpine scenes, which are almost anthropomorphically rendered by the poet. He endeavours to probe the secrets of existence, and regards the universe as the scene of a mighty battle between the inanimate and the living. In Ha-Almoni *('The Anonymous One') he depicts modern man, devoid of ideals and ravaged by spiritual desolation. His poetic cycle* Manginot Yisrael *('Israel Melodies') dwells on Israel's spiritual mission among the nations,* Mahazor Ukraina *('Ukrainian Cycle') depicts the horrors of the pogroms while the cycle* Luhot Genuzim *('Hidden Tablets') is a myth of the development of Juda-ism before the prophetic doctrine exerted its decisive influence.*

The decadence of youth is described in his earlier prose works: Min Ha-Hayim Veha-Mavet *('Of Life and Death') and* Ba-Metzar *('In the Narrow Straits'). The cycle of tales 'People of Shklov' humorously depicts the day-to-day life and cares of the Jews in the Russian Pale of Settlement.*

To the Prophet

What will you here, maker of beauty? In the hearts of these
   merchants and traders you never shall kindle a fire.
When the candle of God is extinguished, the prophet can make it
   His mission
To relight its cold blackened wick.
If there be in the lamp but one oildrop, cast a spark and all is
   Illumined.
But these dead of spirit, O prophet, you never shall light till eternity.
Though all your soul's fire be bared—they'll not raise a flame to eternity.

Do you see how the crowd's making merry? And how many dull
   eyes of glasswork,
And violet faces of women, gleaming and leaning towards you?...
Say not: "I shall conquer and kindle what never before has been
   kindled!"
O prophet!
Suspended in infinite blackness, these coldest and darkest of creatures,
Remnants of matter sprayed out before time from the hand of the
   Maker;
Like blind men they fumble and falter. And at times two collide
   unintentionally
And fumble in the darkness together—
And that is their love...

Then one day there happens among them but one of the world's
   wandering luminaries,
One of those suns that illumine with no thought of reward nor of
   purpose—

Then they shine in the light of his bounty, those creatures all
    drowning in darkness,
Their drear outer cases turn golden, they beam with the joy of the
    simple;
But as soon as the wandering sun passes, their radiance and glory all
    vanish
They remain bits of frozen creation, that know neither pleasure nor
    sorrow,
And they gaze at themselves once again through seven dim eyes of
    obscurity.

What will you here, maker of beauty, in this crowd of merchants and
    traders?
You have shared out your splendour among them—see now how they
    are all drunken!
And you too are drunk and forgetting that you are a sun who must
    wander;
Soon you shall feel the deep yearning, and you'll leave them all, yes
    you'll leave them.
Then the light shall fade from their faces, their fat skin-glory all
    fallen—
Then, sated, your name they'll remember.
And the greasy scales of the butcher shall weigh your soul's deepest
    yearnings,
And graded bushels of grain shall measure your bold imagination,
And rusty shuttles of looms shall spin out the breadth of your
    heartstrings...

Translated by Richard Flantz

The Wrong

Foes are the shades to the sun,
Foes, both the large and the small;
For they hate, without knowing why,
All that's bright and throws them in thrall.

By day the shadows stay hidden
In woods, in dark nooks, out of sight,
Where they lurk and plan secret plots
To destroy the hero of light.

But each time the proud sun breaks through
In scorching scorn to his foes;
His courage is his laughter so warm,
His rays are his arrows and bows.

The trembling shadows all fear
Their conqueror's chains and his glare,
Like negro slaves in revolt
Whose rebellion lies suddenly bare...

Evening, and the sun has grown old,
His light has gone cold, and he's lying—
Sick on his carpet of scarlet,
Helpless and shivering and dying.

Then the slavish shadows charge out,
Wagging tongues of harsh mocking bite;
On their dying foe then they wreak
Their base revenge and their spite.

] 165 [

Scratching and strangling and shoving,
They strike out each trace of his shine;
Like savages and cowards they gouge
The cold dead corpse of the lion.

Then you, O man, stand and look,
Helpless you gaze at the wrong,
Like a dog when he's scented the thieves
And he's bound to his place by the thong.

Translated by Richard Flantz

Pity

Tears stuck in my throat as I ate and a cat approached the house,
Wailing: Man, I don't know you, nor am I able to speak;
From this world's desert I've come to you, god of hunting and fullness!
So give me, pray, of your bread, and no other friend shall I seek.

Or on a day of wild rains and snows, when a sparrow knocks on my
    sill:
Man, your precious warmth without sun... What is your secret way?
For aeons my fathers and I have built and furnished our nests
And have not found your fire. Teach me... I shall do as you say.

And the slaughtered calf hanging by its feet, its neck slit by the knife,
Voicelessly bellowing to the earth: Who has put out my life...
Who has poured my good oil into the coarsest of bottles?
For this decaying flesh—all God's creation throttles.

Translated by Richard Flantz

I do not Wish to Return

Burn all the fields behind me, my passions!
I do not wish to return
To the townships of idylls, that drown
In the mire of medieval and rain-soaked days.
Let the tempest tear down all the bridges of memory!
Lest I be able to return,
For I may lust to return,
Though I be greatly afraid.

And you, evil beings, demons of failure,
With engines of war and iron-shod hooves—
Smash beneath me each rung
That my feet ever trod!
That my escape may be upwards, ever upwards.
I no longer want the return of childhood,
The childhood of the Jewish nation
Oppressed by a nervous father
And strapped by an angry teacher.
Let that be painted by powerless dreamers
And exalted by the outcasts of my day and my age
Who chirrup and cheat.

And let my youth go where it will,
With its drums and its dance of the redskins!
Youth that gleaned gleaming pennies in cities
And lost all its silver;
Whose hunger and sufferings and wandering
Were all but preparations, preparations

For life... What life? It did not come.
Not one tear did I shed for its loss;
And on my deathbed, at the turn of day,
I shall not sigh for its memory.

Leave me but this mature universe:
With the golden sun of its genius,
With this ripe sun—this apple of fire and reason.
Just this world with its glorious anger,
Its merry wisdom and its stuttering
On the brink of great discoveries, or on the brink of hell...
With the blazing heresy, there, at the edge of its skies
And the decline of man so sated with victories
And hungry for the love of unvanquished woman—
Like a precious crown on this my silvering head.
O may you see me so, mounting in flames
Up God's ladder.

Translated by Richard Flantz

Deuteronomy

Yes, I am proud that I am a grandson
To this people who created the book—
Verses and rhymes that will roll, that have rolled
Like broadening waves since binding began.
Broad are the waves,
But measured their chorus that flows in and ebbs;
One wave is swallowed in shimmering depths
And another inherits its chorus,
Carrying it swirling in loud-singing din
To the ear of the listener, to the shore.
Lights pursue shadows,
Laws mingle with song...
And the lay becomes holy.
The poem surpasses the bourns of the tale,
And the sentence the flight of the vision:
Breath and voice and wisps of silence
And voice and wisps of silent breath...
Thus does a great heart beat for his people—
The people of the book from the depths of the ages.
Great and young is this people, this nation of wanderings
In the morning of the world,
That created its law in order to smite
With a flute upon Astartes of sheep.
And as they followed their herds through desert sands and haze,
A jealous God of vengeance revealed himself,
Girt in torches and miracles and voices,
Lowering a mighty head, laughing, admitting:
"You have vanquished me, Israel!"

Yes, great is this people that wrote its laws to music
And its commands to living melodies,
That wove the chains of its heavy decrees
Like the weave of red roses.
How great here the strength, the firm sureness!
And the light of the desert sun is sown.
The verses sound, they flow forth without froth,
Bearing the fate of a primitive people:
Accept, else you drown!
Impassable waters are we to the light-headed,
Dark depths to those who stiffen their necks...
Accept!...

And they flow and they sound and they pass.

So there is reason to suffer, if you are a grandson
To the people who created this book.
For a miracle has occurred here for certain!
From the harsh came forth sweetness,
From the rock of hard sentence, now burst asunder,
Leaped out cascades of plenitude,
And the mark of the stick still appears on the rock...
The words still gush forth, from that day to this,
A worldwide waterfall of life
In the dusts of radiance and incessant melody:
Arise, drink, erring wayfarer, till your soul be sated!
The source will not betray,
The cascade shall not cease.
And I sorrow for this barren world, and am glad
That none of its books are like unto this Book,
And no-one dares to give birth to one similar.

Translated by Richard Flantz

Stop Playing!...

Stop playing with words, young louts!
A wisdom tooth is each true word,
A tooth of pains.
Like an iron screw digging into the flesh,
And there is no aid, no cure and no rest
Till it is violently wrenched out
To its deep flattened root,
Naked and twisting and screaming with pain.
And the man is relieved when it is torn out
And thrown away like a blood-sacrifice
Upon the world's altar.

And for a long time the cured one still licks
The hole of his pains
And swallows his dripping blood.
But the extracted tooth will not grow again,
No healing can help it.
A wisdom tooth shed,
A seer's word said,
Will not grow again
In this world.

He who has sought all his days—
Do not mock "eternal love", wise ones!—
A deep wound is woman,
A rib cut from the body,
Flesh of man and animal,
Taken secretly by God

From manhood in sleep
When, in creation's treasury,
He lacked the materials to finish his work.

And the wounded man roams and roves all his days,
Seeking his stolen flesh
To close the huge open wound,
To stop his outpouring blood—
And he fills his gaping pain
With all that he finds in his travels:
The flowering lily,
Golden tresses and stalks of flax,
Logs of wood and hunks of stone,
Wailing geese and scratching rats...
But there is nothing that will fit the wound...
"Not this!" weeps the man in secret—
Even on conquering and caressing a lioness
His heart weeps: "Not this!..."
And so he errs along the paths of love
Till he falls at the feet of his mate—
Flesh of his flesh and bone of his bone,
But his blood has already died drop by drop
And in the worn-out veins is no fire;
Only then does she fit,
The only one, the pleasant and clear one,
And the wound shuts like a grave.

Translated by Richard Flantz

The Legend of the Duck

[I]

O forest, forest, tell me, do,
I want to know, so teach me:
Why does the wild goose fly so high
On wings that glide, now rising
From swamps and banks of hidden lakes
That rest in shade and ancient moss
And sleep in your dark deepness;
He like a feathered arrow sings
In flashing through blue heavens.
While this goose here, the village-born,
Can only limp from side to side:
"Gag-gag, gag-gag, gag-gag!"
He rises not, nor hovers,
Nor is he ever jealous,
Nor does he budge a wingtip
When his wild brother calls him
Above his head there flying,
Inviting him—"Come southwards"—?

[II]

Well have you seen and asked, my son,
And so, now I shall tell you:
The village goose has sold his wings,
For the price of crumbs he sold them;
His belly grew, became so big;
His wings, they shrunk and shrivelled.
Since then he drags himself along

] 174 [

Each beaten path and gaggles,
And food, just food is all he seeks
While waiting to be slaughtered.
And if he rises now and then
A foot above earth's surface,
In fear, or sighting mighty pools
And remembering distant ages…
His stomach's weight is far too great,
And pulls him down to earth again,
Flat on his nose despite him.
Gag-gag, gag-gag!… It's merciless
And to the ground it binds him.
But my own children, those wild geese
Are masters of their wingspans:
To no one have they sold God's gift—
All flat of belly, broad of wing,
They frolic by my waters.
They scoff at autumn and its cold,
And when it comes they take off,
Like giant arrows sharp of head
They cut through winds and breezes;
Their whistling flight and freedom's sigh
Is heard through all cold heavens.

[III]

And there's a legend among wild geese,
A legend oft repeated:
That once man too knew how to fly—
In early times, long long ago,
He had two wings instead of arms,
Until he learned to eat too much
Of the fruit so sweet and fertile

That the tree of knowledge lavished.
And thus he did from day to day,
Then sated, started laughing:
What good to me are these my wings,
That wave and flap and flutter
Above an empty stomach?
Forgotten then, the conquered spirit
Wailed loud that it was vanquished,
And how it had been so light, aloft,
Between the earth and skyline.
The flesh grew fat from day to day,
The passions too grew heavy—
And then the wingspans withered,
The feathers all began to drop
From off that glorious plumage,
Until they moulted, dried, and turned
To arms and hands and fingers,
So long and thin and fumbling
And dangling down and drooping
Their form upon the stomach;
Inquiring hands, and grasping all,
And digging all the earth up.
And in their helplessness so weak
They made iron their accomplice,
And with it ravaged holy lands
Eternal brothers, taking blood,
And robbing, raping forests.

[IV]

So fell man's pair of mighty wings
That drank the breadths of heaven,
That always, always seek revenge

For their disgrace and downfall;
And with the envy of the flatlands
They shoot up sparks and arrows
At those that fly above them
And try to hunt down every bird
And so enslave it to the earth,
And seek to pluck and make a hand
Of every erring angel's wing.

[v]

And it came to pass across the seas:
A wondrous man was born there,
With wings from shoulders growing,
A dreadful pair, instead of arms,
As once had known his forbears;
He flew and circled in blue skies
In sight of all his teachers,
And there were such that envied him,
And others that had pity:
How shall we cure this flaw of his?
How shall we drag him earthwards?
Let him forget his disease of flight
Let him become one of us,
Not to disturb the people's calm
With din of wings enormous...
Then stones of fields and precious stones
They shot at him, all vainly,
And poisoned arrows and sparks of bronze
Could not restrain his progress.
And then they opened glorious castles,
Luxurious cages, calling:
"Descend now, and inherit!"

He did not fall, nor failed he.
Then women spread their hair to him
Like golden nets of blackest lace...
He did not trust, nor grasped he.

[VI]

And in that place was an evil man,
Who laughed at all their troubles
And thus he spoke: "Give ear to me,
And I alone shall cure him!
Have any seen the fleeting hawk
Not seek his prey below him?
Or a butterfly, in flowery flight,
Not dropping tired, sucking honey
From the yellow plant his brother?
And if a man fly eagle-like,
Will he, up there, amid God's heights
Eat stars as though they're apples?
Or will he drink from teats of clouds
As though he drank from pitchers?
I vow—although he tear apart
The very crowns of planets,
When hungry he'll again descend
To earth—the mother of all stomachs.
In vain you plot to raise your hands
To clip his wings of wonder;
His wings are sacred to the Lord
But his stomach—that is ours:
Let us arise and tempt it!
For it will bring the proud one down,
With all his wings and plumage;
The savage his own wings will break,

And will return on foot, in shame,
To people and to homeland;
Your hands and mine this way stay clean,
So do then as I tell you:
First bolt and bar each doorway here,
Set guards on every garden,
A watch on every fruit-tree.
No man shall ever give him bread,
In neither gift nor purchase;
And children—lovers of all birds—
No crumbs shall dare to throw him,
And youthful women, soft of heart,
Their pitchers shall not give him,
And you shall see the outcome..."

[VII]

And when the winged one came down
To earth, to rest from flying,
He found the wells and gardens barred
With guards around each entrance.
He asked them why, but none replied,
Among his own—a stranger, he,
Among the sleeping, waking,
And hungry among the sated.
Then through strange streets he'd never known
He limped on like an eagle,
His dragging wings a laughing-stock
As he walked erect and fearless.
And so he wandered, a hungry day,
Then two, and three days more,
And home-kept fowls with fat behinds
Clucked out his only solace:

"You've learned to fly! But now pluck out
Those wings of yours so proud,
And then each coop will open wide
Where you can peck contented..."
And loud the scorn of men with arms
That sounded from the windows:
O winged man, now rise and fly
And show us just how high you get
Upon your empty stomach!

[VIII]

The wonder man then shook his head,
Arose, clapped wing to wing,
Tremendous wings of purest white,
And took off to the highest heights,
Contempt in his eyes blazing.
Thus never had he flown before
With swallow's ease and falcon's calm
He plunged up towards the sun.
Among the frozen clouds of ice,
Now lost, now reappearing,
Like a playing arrow, sharp, alive,
Between joints of silver armour.
The evil one then cast a loaf
Of warm bread on the ground;
A basket filled with luscious fruits,
All ripe and red and yellow—
With bluest figs and golden dates—
He spilt them all before him.
The eagle-man beheld this then,
And ravenous hunger gripped him;
He forgot his wings among God's heights,

Remembering but his stomach,
And dived with lack of caution.
Then did the giant wings both break
As he plummetted down to reach the bread
That rolled in dung below him.
Since then he crawls, in hungry shame,
Among the sated armed-men,
And gathers crumbs and leavings.
And his broken wings, encased with dirt,
And his plumage wet with spittings
He drags behind him always...

Translated by Richard Flantz

A Star Fell

A star fell and got lost
In the darkness.
It wasn't noticed. Many stars
Stayed shining up in space.

A tear dropped from my soul
For you, just now.
You won't see it. Many, many
Tears keep falling here below.

Translated by A. C. Jacobs

YAACOV STEINBERG

1887—1947

Poet, story writer and essayist. Born in the Ukraine, he lived in Odessa, Warsaw, Kiev, Switzerland, and from 1914 in Palestine, apart from a few years in Berlin.

His early poems, written in the spirit of the European Decadence, describe the pessimism and solitude of a young individualist who is devoid of any redeeming ideals. His 'Book of Satires' is a series of poems about a world sunk to the lowest degree of degradation, a cynical world of eating, drinking and fornication, while Mecholot ('Dances') speaks of the disillusionment that comes of dreaming. His Eretz-Israel poems, too, express a weariness and a longing for the unattainable; his 'Sonnets of the Café' depict the decay of the city dwellers.

His essays, profoundly and poetically written, deal with contemporary problems, primarily, a negation of the Diaspora and an appraisal of Israel's renaissance in its own country.

On his fiftieth birthday, his collected works were published in three volumes: poems, stories and essays. He also translated into Hebrew works by Daudet, Victor Hugo, Tolstoy and others. Two slim volumes were published posthumously, one devoted to his conversations and the other containing a number of his essays. His collected works appeared in a two-volume edition.

Dances

I have grown tired with looking at white snow
That blots out all colour, and blurs out shape.
Take care. A few more days like this one, and
The whole village will freeze in fatal sleep.

I've lived my life in big, sprawling cities,
But never watched white snow like this come down.
Danger keeps growing, but the villagers
Shut themselves in their houses, sit and yawn.

All the village will be buried in soft snow;
Cold will seal the surface of its grave.
The storm will end, but travellers passing
Won't recognise a place where men once lived.

Translated by A. C. Jacobs

At Night

My love I whispered, by your house at night:
You bent your head, your head of curly hair.
I in sad parables sheathed my delight
And lightly asked love's heavy riddle there.

Then your veil suddenly rustled: you seemed to wait.
Your eyelids trembled a little, as you faced me.
You were like a fish rising toward the bait.
The rustle of secrets moves with it through the sea.

Translated by Dom Moraes

All Of A Summer

My small, my beautiful land, all of a summer
you sat beneath a canopy of blue;
the clinging sea defined your figure clearly
until the storm wind blew.

The storm wind blew; and now you showed your lovers,
as for a breath the blue line disappeared,
a face they had not known—its marvellous changes
born in a storm of tears.

Translated by Robert Friend

Till Evening

Whether to cry or whether to be proud,
I do not know. The change is very strange.
I hold less dear all worldly things, although
their forms become a thousand times more clear.

It is enchantment, deception, or a game,
and like a costly train grows ever longer.
The more my days increase, the more I note
the changes that life brings.

It is a vanity to guess and wonder
about the changeless end of every day:
things have become transparent and remote.
Their shadows move until the daylight fails.

Translated by Robert Friend

Turn Towards the End

Turn towards the end, be a leaf failing—
rottenness gilding it, the stem collapsing.
A faithful crimson gives regret beauty,
a humble withering hints the pride of every death.

Like original sin is the toil of all blooming—
beginning and ending; and life-lust makes muddy
will's every rebellion. Who, twisted or innocent,
ought to disdain then what poverty offers,
and go towards his rest in the yoke of complaining?

Poor, blind the solution; but as the best man, the bridegroom
meekness and solace silently lead him,
and they walk securely on the sad pathway,
beholding all clearly to life's last boundary.

Translated by Robert Friend

Rain at Night

In the heart of night, in winter, there was this hour:
suddenly down on the earth poured the strong rain—
and in its mouth the language of riddle and truth.

Magnificent rain of ever-increasing power,
with streams of an abundance never ending,
the many streams all blending in one song.

And when its plenitude approached past midnight,
night's secret hour where sound no longer dwells,
the ultimate boundary of silence between yesterday and tomorrow,

the rain grew troubled, flowing and rising in flood,
running its pure way from the living temple of heaven,
like a messenger from on high bringing the word of God.

Translated by Robert Friend

It has Been Long...

It has been long since first my fears grew light.
My stubbornness in the ordeal cast off its dross,
the whole of my soul concealed death's nakedness.

Much has been shown me. Many can testify,
among good men and bad, that I
now kneel before the humble and the poor,
who once looked down at them from a proud height;

that I behold again the magic boundary
between those brothers: the future and happiness,
without lips' pride, without an armor for my nakedness.

I have striven long with many of the abashed
to find this refuge, where we need no longer fear
the weeping of our flesh, its hidden truth.

Translated by Robert Friend

I. Z. RIMON

1889—1958

Poet. Born in Bison, Poland. He studied at yeshivot. In 1909 he came to Palestine, where he worked first as secretary of a charitable organization, and later as a teacher and librarian. For three years he retired to the seclusion of the Synagogue of the Ari (illustrious kabbalist) in Safed, and later went to Jerusalem, where he was profoundly influenced by Chief Rabbi Kook. His work is charged with the profound religious feeling of a man who senses God in all life's appearances. Yet erotic notes mingle with these religious feelings and with the craving for a revelation of God, whom the poet invests with the attributes of an artist, the world being His creation.

His selections of poems include: Leket *('Collection'),* Devir *('Holy Temple'),* BeMahaze *('In the Vision') and* Ketarim *('Crowns'). He also wrote commentaries on Isaiah, Jeremiah, Ezekiel, Hosea and Amos, and an appreciation of Rabbi Kook, 'The Poet of Judaism'.*

I Shall Shear My Crown

I shall shear my crown, my head's own glory, and say to God:
I shall no more come to the mountains,
I shall no more climb their summits
To seek your echo there.

Nor secret caves shall I search
To seek your steps,
For you have poured splendour also on to nearby fields,
On to every flowering tree.
There is no splendour but your splendour.

Why shall I dwell in the mountains,
I shall live in the wilderness—
And you cast joy on every path,
And on every path you are!...

Translated by Richard Flantz

God Lives!

God lives! The splendour of the skies says so,
And the black storm that hides them also speaks;
God lives! The ornament of earth says so,
And the tempest uprooting forests also speaks;
God lives! The day in its brilliance says so,
And the night with its terrors also speaks;
God lives! The purity of rivers says so,
And the heavy burden of fog also speaks;
God lives! The rich crop of mountains says so,
And the gushing flow of lava also speaks;
God lives! Life in its spring says so,
And death that is cruel also speaks;
God lives! The sea in frothing waves says so,
And in its whispered yearnings also speaks;
God lives! My heart, alien but bursting, says so,
And flowing into God's lap also speaks.

Translated by Richard Flantz

A Sea Arose to Greet Me

[I]

A sea arose to greet me and the song of its waves gripped the skies;
Gold drips upon my path, in earthly glory I rejoice.
I have been filled with a vision since long ago,
My vision shall grow, for I grow in its glory!

Beat, my sea, your waves! Raise your blue to my eyes!
Behold, the skies will yet deepen,
My heart shall cross the law of its shores—
Is that why you rage then, O sea?
I shall kick at the skies and their golden stars,
The song of my abandoned youth shall rise again in my heart.
Where is a border to my soul and a God within—
I shall move in it like a drunk
With my new bursting passions!
Only to a whorehouse will I not go, nor to a woman give my vigour,
Lest I ravish the holiness,
And lose the glory of my song,
For my song is my life!

[II]

My heart erupted and I did not hear its voice; a wall of gold enclosed it,
And my vision embraced the skies, and I did not know my spirit,
For the hand of my God overcame me...
I wanted to touch a woman's hair
By the light of burning suns—
And he held my hand, whispering words of love:
Wait just a little, with your chastity you shall conquer,

Flames of the abyss shall redden your steps,
Harps of the skies shall burst round your head—
Your heart shall be like God...
Why sink? Rise, like the sun, rise yet higher...
Sing to me of love, like Halevi, like Ibn Gvirol tie crowns to my soul,
The prophecy goes, the vision of God comes—
With God in the holiness!

Woe is me, that I believed... woe, that my heart quakes with noise...
I knew that early and late would conflict—
And my God's in the holy flames!
Wife! Your beauty deepens, what will you dream?
On your finger will flower the ring
Of my love,
I shall wind like a snake around you,
And if I be a lion, from your hand I'll eat hay...

Grant me your beauty, grant me your grace more...
Tell me, my sister: Whence is the gold,
And why does my heart long for it so?
I shall mould my soul on expanses
And with my blood redden the earth,
For I have grown rich.

Woe is me, that love has passed from me!
I shall kiss you as you command and kiss again,
And if God stands in my doorway...
I am a son of the times, whose idea sullied my youth;
I am made up of my afflictions.
Now I shall fall on the fire of the vision of God,
And perish in its flames!...

Translated by Richard Flantz

For a Girl's Tresses

For a girl's tresses God burns in longing
And is not ashamed.
He has left the hermit's haven,
And strains for the breadths of scarlet—
Will you lust like a man, O God?!...
You gleam like a male—
You have been as bad as I, a man!
Let me hound you now,
For you have hounded me,
Eternal God, O love!...

Translated by Richard Flantz

I Have Learned to Mould

I have learned to mould and sculpt in matter,
And to pour the lights of the soul.
On the heights of mountain summits
Stands the princess,
Her body moulded in marble.
All glory gleams from her sculpted eyes,
Till grace dissolves in fainting.
The sun of Jerusalem shone on her…
Terribly did I burn and yearn for her,
And I long for her still…
And she called in her pride: "He who sings my song,
His shall I be!…"
Now I shall go, now I shall come, and say:
"I have learned your song, here it is in my mouth:
Your body is fairer than the marble of skies,
O daughter of kings,
And the radiance of your eyes than the radiance of souls;
With prayer and fasting have I discovered your secret—
Be mine!…"

Translated by Richard Flantz

RACHEL

1890—1931

Poet. Born in Viatka, Russia, she went to a Russian high school, wrote her early poems in Russian, and studied art in Kiev. She went to Palestine in 1909 and worked as a farm labourer at Rehovot, and later at Kinneret. She was greatly influenced by A. D. Gordon. In 1913, she went to France and later to Russia, where she taught. Returning to Palestine in 1919, she became a member of the Kevutzah of Degania. In her latter years, she suffered from consumption, and the knowledge of her approaching death is reflected in her poems. She wrote simple, sensitive lyrics charged with delicate symbols and imbued with a love for the countryside and nature. Many of her poems have been put to music.

Her poetical works include: Saphiah *('After-growth'),* Mineged *('From Opposite'),* Nevo *('Mt. Nebo') and translations into Hebrew of poems by Anna Akhmatova, Charles van Leerberg and Francis Jame. Her collected poems appeared as* Shirat Rahel *('The Poetry of Rahel').*

Perhaps

Perhaps it was never so.
Perhaps
I never woke early and went to the fields
To labour in the sweat of my brow.

Nor in the long, blazing days
Of harvest
On top of the wagon, laden with sheaves,
Made my voice rise in song.

Nor bathed myself clean in the calm
Blue water
Of my Kineret, O, my Kineret,
Were you there or did I only dream?

Translated by A. C. Jacobs

Michal

And Michal Saul's daughter loved David—
and she despised him in her heart.

Though years divide, we're sisters yet;
Your vineyard stands though weeds invade;
Still tinkle anklet, amulet;
Your red silk garment does not fade.

By a small window still you stand,
Proud, but a death within your eyes.
My sister, I can understand—
Who also love whom I despise.

Translated by Robert Friend

Elijah

My room is like Elijah's, a high attic,
and sometimes there comes into my head
the thought of that miraculous old man—
how he revived the dead.

Seven times he stretched out on the child,
the voice of his unending prayer cried to the Lord.
At last he sat by the mourning mother and said:
"Your son is restored."

My dear dead! He won't come as before,
to pray—outstretched—with burning lips and eyes.
No voice cries out. None listens. You are cold.
And you will never rise.

Translated by Robert Friend

I

Quiet as lake water—
this is the way I am—
fond of children's eyes, daily tranquillities,
the poems of Francis Jammes.

Long ago my soul wore purple;
I wandered on the peaks,
one with the large winds
and eagles' shrieks.

Long ago… but that was long ago.
Times
change. And now—
this is the way I am.

Translated by Robert Friend

Revolt

Like a bird in the *shochet's** palm you flutter in my hand,
insolent pride.
I stop your mouth,
I press together the wings of your back,
and I laugh at you.
I've got you at last.
This is revenge for the flowers you plucked in their early bloom,
for your fences that cut off my path,
for the world whose rainbow colours you made dim.
Lie down in your corner of darkness till I return,
till I return from him.

Translated by Robert Friend

*ritual slaughterer

My Dead

Only the dead won't die

Only they are left me; they are faithful still
Whom death's sharpest knife can no longer kill.

At the turn of the highway, at the close of day
They silently surround me; they quietly go my way.

A true pact is ours, a tie time cannot dissever.
Only what I have lost is what I possess forever.

Translated by Robert Friend

His Wife

She turns and calls him by name
With the voice of every day.
How can I trust my voice
Not to give me away?

In the street, in the full light of day,
She walks by his side.
I in the dark of the night
Must hide.

Bright and serene on her hand
Is her ring of gold.
The iron fetters I wear
Are stronger, seven fold.

Translated by Robert Friend

I Have only Known how to Tell of Myself

I have only known how to tell of myself.
My world is like the ant's; my pack
Is just as much a burden to me,
Too heavy by far for my frail back.

My way, like the ant's to the top of the tree,
Is a laboring way, a painful way,
That hands of giants have mockingly blocked,
Hands with practical jokes to play.

All my paths twist, are wet with tears
Because of my fears of a giant hand.
Distant beacons, you have deceived me.
Why did you call me, miraculous land?

Translated by Robert Friend

The Permitted there is and the Forbidden...

The longing fire devours
The strands I have carefully braided;
Like the sun that draws up flowers,
The gift of tenderness lures me.

My soul, hunched over the sorrow
Of my life and death, stands bare.
O do not stare at me,
At the disgrace of my poverty.

Translated by Robert Friend

My Strength Grows Less and Less...

My strength grows less and less.
Be good to me, be good to me! Be
my narrow bridge across a sad abyss, across the sadness of my days.
Be good to me, be good to me! Something of soul.
Be my heart's prop.
In the waste places be a shade-giving tree.
Be good to me!
The night is long, the dawn is far away.
Be a small light, be sudden joy,
be my daily bread!

Translated by Robert Friend

Day of Good Tidings

And there were four leprous men at the entering in
of the gate: and they said one to another: . . .
. . .this day is a day of good tidings.

II. Kings, 7:3-9

Long ago, on a day when Samaria lay
   Under siege by the terrible foe,
Four messengers came to pronounce freedom's name,
   Four lepers like snow.

Samaria then. Now hunger eats men
   In our land, north and south;
But I should not desire a message of fire
   If it came from a leper's mouth.

The pure bring the cure, the pure will redeem.
   If redemption is not in their power,
I choose then to fall from the fortress wall
   When the messengers come in their hour.

Translated by Robert Friend

ISRAEL EFROS

1891—

*Poet, Judaic scholar and philosopher. Born in Ostrog, Poland, he studied
at Mir Yeshiva in Lithuania, emigrated with his family to the United
States in 1905, and studied at the Rabbi Yitzhak Elhanan Yeshiva in New
York, the New York University (B. A., 1913) and Columbia University
(M. A., 1914, Ph. D., 1915). He founded the Hebrew College and Teachers'
Training College in Baltimore (1918), was Professor of Hebrew at Buffalo
University (1929-1941) and at Hunter College, New York (1941-1955),
and Professor of Jewish Philosophy and Hebrew Literature at Dropsie
College, Philadelphia. In 1955, Efros settled in Israel as first rector of
Tel Aviv University and has been honorary President of the University since
1960.*

*His first poems were published in 1912, and since then have appeared in
Hebrew periodicals in America and other countries. He is the author of
studies, in Hebrew and English, in ancient and mediaeval Jewish philosophy,
and co-author of a large standard English-Hebrew dictionary (1929, with
many reprintings).*

His Hebrew works include: Poems (1932); Wigwamim Shotekim
('Silent Wigwams', on the life of the American Indians, 1933); Zahav
('Gold', on the 1849 gold rush, 1942); Anahnu Hador *('We are the Generation', collected poems, 1945);* Zacharti Lach *('I Remember Thee',
1950);* Goral Uphitom *('Fate and Suddenness', 1954);* HaPilosophia
HaYehudit Ha-Atika *('Ancient Jewish Philosophy', 1959);* Ben Hupim
Nistarim *('Between Hidden Shores', poems, 1961). Has translated into
Hebrew Shakespeare's 'Hamlet', 'Timon of Athens' and 'Coriolanus', and
much of Bialik's poetry into English (1948). He published serially an account
of his visits to post-war displaced-persons camps in the weekly 'Hadoar',
later appearing in Yiddish translation in book form (Buenos Aires, 1947).*

*His works in English include: The Problem of Space in Jewish Mediaeval
Philosophy (1917); The Bloody Jest, a Drama (1922); Philosophical
Terms in the* More Nevukhim *(Maimonides' 'Guide to the Perplexed')
(1924); Maimonides' Treatise on Logic (1938).*

Tree

Man never knows the roots he has struck
Till the time he is plucked.

Till he is suddenly tugged with a pair of tongs
From the soil where he grew all along.

Then the cry of his roots, shrill and erect,
Is like the cry of a soul when its shanty is wrecked.

And as when teeth are slowly extracted
His firm flesh will have quaked and contracted.

Then silence, and soon he'll be praying anew
In another soil for rain and for dew.

But a ring of shudders which years didn't form
Is the heirloom within from that night of storm.

Translated by Abraham Birman

The Ship

[I]

An open amazement, radiant, blue,
Amid black waves under the moon's canopy,
And enclosed with no symbol or sign by a circle of silence.

But the pull of my ship toward an invisible point
Is mighty and sharp
Like the force of celestial spheres.

Is my way, too, embossed
In this marble amazement
And carved by the balance of worlds?

Or is it my heart, my stormy bird,
That impels from within you, my ship?

[II]

Now I am ancient,
More ancient than the chain of my forbears.

Now I am so young, younger
Than my grandson's grandson.

Now the graves open up,
Ghosts march in procession,
The last generation awakes in its cradle.

And I am a ship for them all,
A vessel for setting aright
A fearful mistake.

[III]

I am but a starry point wriggling in space.
Arise, crack it up like a kernel
Or press it against your ear like a conch.
What will you see? What will you hear?

Multitudes, multitudes,
Roaring like billows beneath me—
What turmoils the nether world?

Heads on heads coming up from behind,
Still veiled by the sleep of the moon.

My step, my step—
What depths in commotion,
What a long train of distant souls.

Translated by Abraham Birman

On the Sea Shore

From where have you come? From the flame and bereavement?
From a soil that has turned into fiery coals?—
No, brother, my country—Love's deepest achievement—
Stretched out, green and lush with its well-watered knolls.

Perhaps from the venomous, serpentine creatures
That slither in fairest of groves and in grass—
No, brother, I happened to see godlike features
On man's earthly face when I saw him pass.

Or fear of the End, a light cloud as a token,
The vision of Daniel on the river Ulai?—
No, brother, if ever the heavens split open,
Alas here too for the young wheat and the rye.

Then why did you join us? We've nothing but utter
Starvation and labour and tears to bequeath?—
Bewildered I smiled, my heart all a-flutter
With joy and alarm and a secret beneath.

Translated by Abraham Birman

In the Month of Ziv*

When in the month of Ziv you tour the land,
Up to Jerusalem or Galilee,
A burnished bloom will lie on the brown sand
And greenish pastures like a golden sea.

And twinkling flames will everywhere enfold
With graceful impudence the stalk's attire,
Till the whole field become like Moses' bowl:
All gold and living coals, all gold and fire.

When in the month of Ziv you tour this land,
Be glad even though the tints are much aglare—
For all you see rose yesterday from sand
With God's mighty name still blazing there.

Translated by Abraham Birman

*Ziv—the old Hebrew name for the month of Iyar, roughly
corresponding to the calendar month of May. The word
'Ziv' means brightness.

DAVID FOGEL

1891—1943?

*Poet and novelist. Born in Podolia, Russia, he roamed through various
towns in Galicia, arriving in 1912 in Vienna, where he stayed till 1925. He
then lived in Palestine for two years, after which he went to Berlin and
thence to Paris. He was captured by the Nazis in 1943 and sent to a con-
centration camp where he perished.*

His collection of short poems, Lifney ha-Shaar he-Afel *('Before the
Dark Gate'), constitutes an expressionistic rendering of a mood. They
bring out the anguish of the individual, alone in the great city, ever aware
of the Gate of Death looming up before him. His verse is marked by the
symbolism of colours, simplicity of language, freely constructed stanzas,
and the blank verse charged with a rhythm closely fitted to the contents.*

His novelette BeVet haMarpeh *('In the Sanatorium') portrays life at a
TB sanatorium in Austria and stresses the erotic desire of the patients.*

His novel Hayey Nesuim *('Married Life') is the tragedy of an as-
similated Jew, who squanders his life in his infatuation for a loose-living
baroness. It describes the crushing boredom and emptiness of family life
in a large city.*

He translated Hauptmann's 'Der Ketler von Soana'.

If Night Nears Your Window

If night nears your window,
In nakedness come out to him.

He'll ripple softly, he'll darken
Round your still beauty,
Touching the tips of your breasts.

I'll stand, a lost traveller, with him,
And quietly we'll both feel desire.
Come to us, who are both darkling:

Your two eyes shall travel before
Us, to light
The way for me and my friend.

Translated by Dom Moraes

On my pale Couch, my Body

On my pale couch, my body
In nakedness shines silently
Like white fire.

And the night of my hair,
A dark waterfall, floats free
To the weft of the rug.

Come, my lover.
Virgin, my beauty forever
Burns for the blue of your eyes.

Come...

It deepens, the red of my walls.

And the dusk, solitary,
Nears my couch,
And spreads a black dress
Over me.

And the two glimmering streams
Of my feet
I shall no longer see.
I cry, it is dark...

Translated by Dom Moraes

Silently You Stand Before Me...

Silently you stand before me,
your azure gaze
passes me sadly,
floats towards the horizon.

Where are you sending your soul?
Not yet do your longings
flutter around me
like brilliant butterflies.

A wanderer now, you are going from me.
But your crooked staff
will guide you.

And when your feet are treading the far wood
your quiet footsteps
in my yearning soul
will rustle silently.
Rustle endlessly.

Translated by Robert Friend

With Gentle Fingers

With gentle fingers,
the rain is playing
a secret, sorrowful melody
on the black organ of night.

Now in the dark we sit
each in his home
—the children have fallen asleep—
silent, to hear the rain
because it tells of our sadness.

Our mouths no longer have the words;
our feet are weary
with the day;
no dance in them anymore.

Translated by Robert Friend

On Autumn Nights

On autumn nights
a leaf falls in the woods unseen,
lies silently on the ground.

A fish leaps from the waters
of a stream,
and in the dark
a flapping wetness echoes.

In the black distance are sown
hoofbeats of horses unseen,
dissolving.

All this
the weary wanderer hears
and trembles in his bones.

Translated by Robert Friend

Waiting Rooms

Heavy curtains in the waiting rooms
of famous doctors drape the windows like a pall;
no distant murmur of men ascends to them,
no rattle of wagons from the streets below.

Around the room pictures of long ago
gaze darkly; statues freeze before they spring.
Deep is the red of cupboard and of wall;
an ancient silence covers everything.

A man drowns in these heavy silences,
lost in the chair's upholstery, a light put out,
an object like the objects all about.

But when on the softness of rugs a step draws near,
a shiver goes through him, shakes him out of his ease.
He stares at the doctor with great bulging eyes.

Translated by Robert Friend

A Single Carriage

A single—the last—carriage is ready for the journey;
let us mount and start,
because it will not wait.

I've seen young girls depart,
their narrow faces
flushed and mournful
like scarlet sunsets;

and round and rosy children
who left in their innocence
simply because they were called.

And I've seen men
who walked proud and tall through the streets of the world,
their large eyes projecting far
from where they stood—
they, too, got on the carriage leisurely
and are gone.

We are the last,
the day is ending,
a single—the last—carriage is ready for its journey.
Let us mount quietly
and start—we, too—
because it will not wait.

Translated by Robert Friend

] 231 [

ESTHER RAAB

1893—

Poet. Born in Petah Tikva in 1899, she attended a teachers' training
college and worked at farming and as a teacher.

Her poems are distinctly lyrical; their themes: Israel's landscape and
man merging with it. Though short in form, her lyrics have a highly-
polished artistic style.

Collected poems: Kimshonim *('Thistles', 1930), and "The Poems of*
Esther Raab" (1965).

Serenade for Two Poplars

Tonight I had a rendezvous
With two exalted poplars
And one lofty palm-tree.
The human habitats beneath them
Are also cosy and warm,
Bustling like beehives.
But I
Feel good tonight
With two exalted poplars
And one lofty palm-tree
With light clouds on their tops;
The smell of medlar in the hedges,
Shadows on the asphalt.

Translated by Abraham Birman

The Eruption of Thistles

Thistles erupted in the standing corn,
Spilling like milk
On the face of the earth.
At night the moon will lap up
Milky saucers swaying
On thin stalks,
And clouds, leaving white trails behind,
Will dip into the froth of
Blooming, flowering thistles,
And swarms of bee-eaters
Will gurgle and frolic
And fill their little bellies
Fom white thistle-saucers
Alive with insects.
The screw-beans have closed on the thistle
Lest the sand, too, be engulfed.
The smell of soft, liquid screw-beans
And the sharp, pungent odour of thistles
Nestling close to each other
Will fill the wide gaps
In the shallow clods.

Translated by Abraham Birman

Holy Grandmothers in Jerusalem

Holy grandmothers in Jerusalem,
May your virtue protect me.
The smell of blossoms and blooming orchards
I suckled with my mother's milk.
Feet soft as hands, fumbling
In the torrid sand,
And tousled eucalypti
Laden with bees and hornets
Whispered a lullaby to me.
Seven times shall I steep myself
Into the Mediterranean
To prepare for King David, my beloved,
And I shall go up to him, with glorious dignity,
To the mountains of Jerusalem;
I shall sit with Deborah under the date-tree,
Have coffe with her and talk
About war and defence.
Holy grandmothers in Jerusalem,
May your virtue protect me.
I can feel the smell of your garments,
The aroma of Sabbath-candles and naphthaline.

Translated by Abraham Birman

Like a Dead Bird

Like a dead bird
Upon the stream
You floated towards me.
Your upturned eyes were still,
Flickering for a moment.
Though the lustreless gold
Your arms were tired,
Imparting sorrow.
A meagre olive-tree above us,
Pale shadows at our feet.

Translated by Abraham Birman

Two Vultures and One Fig-Tree

Two vultures
And one fig-tree
Are hanging on naught
Vertiginously.
Between clouds and pines.
Doors—seaward—
And gates—skyward—
Are agape.
The rustle of flight wings,
A multitude of greenery
Like the murmur of holy
Brooks.
Two vultures
And one fig-tree
Are hanging
On naught.

Translated by Abraham Birman

YESHURUN KESHET

1894—

Poet, critic and essayist. Born in Minsk-Mazowiecz, Poland, he went to Palestine in 1911 and taught in Jaffa. Returning to Europe, he taught at a Jewish secondary school in Lithuania, studied philosophy, philology and the history of art at Rome, Berlin and Paris, and settled in Palestine in 1927.

His poetry which is elegiac and reflective, offers a combination of the lyrical and the epic; it is restrained, tending to the abstract and to purity of form. It stresses the vacuity of life, the sense of loneliness borne by the man who dreams, who knows only too well that his yearning for the sun will be enveloped by the darkness of night; it reveals an aesthetic approach to nature and a romantic conception of woman.

His literary essays endeavour to bring out the synthesis that exists between the personality of the writer and the elements of his creative work. They set out to explain literary manifestations in the light of the writers' biographical background and appraise the Jewish impact on spiritual phenomena in world culture.

His works include collected poems: Ha-Helech ba-Aretz *('The Wayfarer in the Land')* and Ha-Hayim ha-Genuzim *('The Hidden Life'),* essays and literary criticism: Ha-Derech ha-Ne'elama *('The Invisible Road'),* Be-Doro shel Bialik *('In the Generation of Bialik'),* Be-Dor Oleh *('In the Rising Generation)',* Maskiyot *('Images'),* Shirat ha-Mikra *('Poetry of the Bible'),* Ruhot ha-Maarav *('Winds from the West'),* and Havdalot *('Distinctions').*

He has translated into Hebrew works by Romain Rolland, Thomas Mann, Montaigne, William James, Kafka, Gerhart Hauptmann, H.G. Wells, Strindberg, Pascal and others.

Cypresses

At the sky-edge walking,
At the edge of evening,
Cypresses, exiles;

Too dumb to reveal,
Too proud to conceal
Their loneliness' secret...

Black angels they are,
Folding their wings,
First heralds of night,—

Fading and glimmering,
Trailing gold;
Dark their beginnings

At dusk, at dusk.

Translated by Robert Friend

Swallows Over Kinneret

At the close of day, over the roofs of the town
how frenzied is the swallows' final flight.
They darken the red sky as they whirl down
their tipsy whistling from the edge of night.

How they storm there, rage and swoop and soar
in branching flight until the last of brightness.
Withdraw, Darkness. Theirs is not song but light;
their vigour of life grows strong in your despite.

They welcome the god of freedom, shadow without
rebellion. Day's death has made these swallows
doubly proud. If I like them could fly
across night's threshold, my soul would grow
inebriate with freedom when death came.
O drink the distances. Fly, sing, my soul.
Now that the end's come, amplify your light.

Translated by Robert Friend

On Parting

It is evening, my soul, and the heavens
Will give you a last look of grace.
The Garden of God lightens up, flushed with joy,
Encircled by overawed mountains.
A hood of perennial snow in the distance,
Unsullied like dreams of our youth.
A sweet, golden secret
The almond shall whisper to reddening peaches
And vine-tendrils, naked, will shed faithful tears
Down the hill's humble slope
Till it seem that the soul is still pure,
That virtue can thrive outside man,
Intact to the end, unabated, unmarred
And doubly resplendent at death.

Behold, an invisible hand has displayed
A tentative sceptre of fire
On the tractable meadow of spring:
A merciful, tangible sign...
I know you, good envoy. You fooled me, but soon
Your fraud has become a salvation, a marvellous path
To hosts of enigmas, a comforting trail
To footsteps of wonder.
O highway that ransoms the heart and engulfs it away—
All my life I have chased you, as if I were shown
A pathway uncharted by Heaven,
As if Earth were false and your gospel alone were the true one.
And you, with the touch of a sorcerer's wand,

Transmuted my flesh into God and my thoughts into Joy.
I trusted and trusted. I ran after you
When you pulled me, but my outstretched hand
Embraced a dark void, an embroidered chimera,
Ephemeral, transient forms.
The Entity thrives and my life is intact
But vision and happiness perish.
To flare up like fire, go out like a shadow—
This is your way, O beauty!
A billow of darkness that flows
To hidden matutinal shores
Will come roaring over my head
And then you will lose me, my soul.
The aureate sceptre will beckon me still,
The face of the earth shine with candour;
But I'll bury my face in my hands
Not to see, not to heighten the pain,
And wilfully lower my eyes
To what *is*,
To turpitude, wickedness, lies...
What boots it to tempt with your last faded charm
A heart proud and broken
At dusk?
No vision nor emptiness. Let me be silent,
My soul, with my eloquence gone,
And speechless behold you before
We part.
It is evening, my soul,
It is evening.

Translated by Abraham Birman

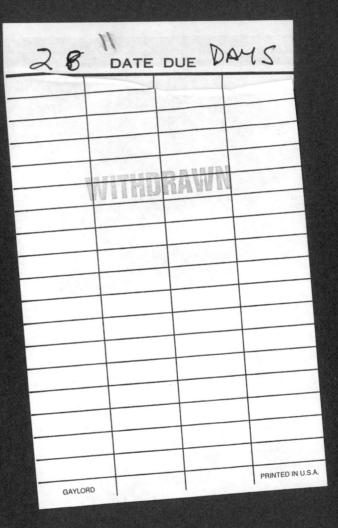